THEY CALL
IT MURDER

A Play

BETTINE MANKTELOW

SAMUEL   FRENCH

LONDON

NEW YORK   TORONTO   SYDNEY   HOLLYWOOD

Please note our NEW ADDRESS:

Samuel French Ltd
52 Fitzroy Street London W1P 6JR
Tel: 01 - 387 9373

THEY CALL IT MURDER

First presented by Howard Theatre Productions at the
Leas Pavilion, Folkestone, in July 1976, with the
following cast of characters:

Peggy Strange	Jill Hope
Babs Strange	Catherine Crewe
Julie Strange	Emma Sutton
Howard Pierce	Michael Rooney
Julian Fudge	Clive Johnstone
Mr Dalrymple	Peter Harding
Mrs Moore	Morrar Kennedy

The Play directed by Robert Howard
Designed by Imogen Magnus

The action takes place in the living-cum-dining-room of
a lower middle-class household in a dockside town

Time—the present

AUTHOR'S NOTE

The play can be played in three acts or, if preferred, in two acts with the interval coming at the end of Act II, Scene 1.

The three girls are poorly off financially, but are well spoken, well educated and well dressed. Because of their circumstances they are condemned to live in genteel poverty, but they do not belong to that environment. Only Mrs Moore and, to a lesser extent, Howard, are what used to be called "working class".

ACT I

Scene 1

The living-cum-dining-room of a lower middle-class household in a dockside town. Late afternoon, September

The room is poorly furnished. There are two doors, one to the hall and the other to the kitchen. Below the kitchen door is the fireplace. There are two armchairs, sideboard, dining-table with chairs, a small settee. Opposite the fireplace is a window. (See the plan of the set on page 61)

As the Curtain *rises, Mrs Moore is coming from the kitchen in her outdoor clothes. She is a middle-aged to elderly woman "what does" for the family; rather garrulous, cheerful and unpretentious. Julia Strange enters from the hall, wearing a summer dress and cardigan, carrying her handbag. She is aged eighteen, a bright, intelligent, attractive and unsophisticated girl*

Mrs Moore Oh, I thought I heard the door. I'm glad it's you. I just popped in with the fish. I promised Peggy I'd get some for your tea. It's on the kitchen table.

Julie Thanks, Mrs M. You are kind. (*She sits in an armchair and kicks off her shoes*) I *am* tired.

Mrs Moore Poor old thing! Doesn't suit you waiting on tables, does it? I wish I could stay and make you a cup of tea but I have to get my Charlie's dinner. It puts him in a bad mood if I'm late.

Julie That's all right, Mrs M. It's good of you to come in at all.

Mrs Moore The way I look at it, dear, if you can't do a good turn for somebody once in a while what can you do? Anyway, I do it for your dear mother's sake, rest her soul, as much as anything. That old man in there is too much for you to look after, and him on his deathbed. A cussed old devil, he is and no mistake. Swore at the doctor this morning he did just because he was late. Still, the doctor swore back. He's an old bugger he said to me, and I had to agree.

Julie He's always been very obstinate.

Mrs Moore He has that. Ruled your mother with a rod of iron and then you girls. Still, you've done well for yourselves all of you, but especially you, Julie. What do you think of your granddaughter going to Cambridge I said to him when I heard you'd passed.

Julie What did he say?

Mrs Moore Said it was what he expected of you and woe betide you if you hadn't—that's what.

Julie That sounds like him. He hasn't once praised me or said he's pleased about it. A little practical appreciation wouldn't come amiss what's more!

Mrs Moore Yes, I see what you mean. I said to my Charlie it's a crying shame you 'aving to work in a café during your holidays, a girl like you! And with the money the old boy's got stashed away.

Julie He says that's how he got it—by not giving it up to the poor and needy!

Mrs Moore Old miser! It won't do him no good when he's dead! (*She looks at the clock*) Oh, Lord, look at the time! I must be off . . . (*She moves to the hall, and then stops*) Oh dear, I nearly forgot what with talking and everything. Those pills . . .

Julie What pills?

Mrs Moore The doctor left some new pills for the old man. They're on the mantelpiece in there. He said the old man is to have them if he has another attack, like, they could save his life, he said, so be sure to remember.

Julie All right, I'll remember. 'Bye then.

Mrs Moore Good-bye, dear. I'll be in again tomorrow. Just leave a list out for the shopping.

Mrs Moore exits to the hall

Julie O.K. 'Bye!

The front door slams. Julie sighs and closes her eyes. After a moment banging commences off, and a voice raised, the old man calling out: "Somebody there? Who's there? I want something." The banging continues—a heavy stick on the floor

(*Rising wearily*) All right, Grandad, I'm coming.

Julie exits to the hall

Muffled voices can be heard off

Julie (*off*) What do you want?

Grandad (*off*) A hot-water bottle and be quick about it.

Julie (*off*) But it isn't cold today, Grandad.

Grandad (*off*) It's cold in 'ere.

Julie (*off*) Oh, all right. I won't be long.

Grandad (*off*) And I want a cup of tea while you're about it.

Julie (*off*) I'll be making the tea soon for all of us.

Grandad (*off*) I mean now, not bloody next week some time.

Julie (*off*) Yes, all right.

Julie returns, looking depressed, and goes off to the kitchen. Babs Strange enters from the hall, in a dressing-gown and yawning. She is a nurse, aged twenty-five; a bit of a nymphomaniac, loves good times, amusing, attractive, practical and honest. She sits in an armchair and gets out her cigarettes. Julie returns

Babs God, what is going on? He woke me up with all that banging.

Julie He said he was cold. I'm sorry he disturbed you. I just didn't get in there quickly enough. He wants a hot-water bottle and a cup of tea.

Babs (*yawning*) I could have done with another half-an-hour. Never mind, I'm up now. (*She stretches*) And I'm nights off tonight, whoopee!

Julie I just don't know how you can bear being on permanent night duty!

Babs I couldn't bear being on permanent day duty, duckie, not with those crabby old sisters breathing down my neck. You'll escape all that, at least, some marvellous top job for you when you leave Cambridge—you'll see!

Julie (*dubiously*) I wonder.

Babs No doubt about it.

Julie I must say I wouldn't want to be a waitress all my life. Oh, my aching feet! (*She sits on the arm of Babs's chair and massages her calves*)

Babs Waitresses and nurses, dear, all develop varicose veins and fallen arches, it's an occupational hazard. Have a good soak in the bath and you'll feel better. Only bags I the bathroom first. I've got a hot date tonight!

Julie Who is it this time?

Babs You know—Swami, the Orthopaedic Registrar.

Julie Oh yes, that's right. Dr Swamananda, your Ceylonese heart-throb! I can't remember when you last went out with an English doctor.

Babs I can't remember when I last met an English doctor, not at our hospital anyway.

Julie Still, you're never short of boyfriends, wherever they come from.

Babs I often wonder why. I suppose it's my availability!

Julie Don't undervalue yourself.

Babs I don't. I know what I want out of life, and it isn't a long, dull engagement followed by an even longer, duller marriage such as my elder sister seems to want. I'm just a happy hedonist! A short life and a gay one, that's my motto.

Julie You certainly work at it!

Babs That sounds like criticism.

Julie No, I didn't mean it like that—only you're always getting at Peggy, and she's put up with so much.

Babs Yes, us for one thing, and Grandad for another. I'm not saying she isn't a saint, but like all saints she can't help resenting it a bit. Anyway, she's got her whipping-boy—dear, dull old Howard!

Julie Poor Howard!

A kettle whistles in the kitchen

Babs Thar she blows!

Julie I'll see to it. I'll do his hot-water bottle first and then put the kettle on again for tea.

Julie exits to the kitchen

Babs O.K. (*She rises and goes to look at herself in the mirror over the mantelpiece*) What a sight!

Peggy Strange enters from the hall carrying some shopping in a basket. She is aged thirty-two, and works in a bank; a rather inhibited young woman who worries about appearances and what people think. She has spent her life largely doing things she did not want to do. She is in a state of tension with domestic problems, is nervous and overwrought; nice-looking but very conservative in dress and repressed in manner; to tally different from her sisters

Peggy Oh hallo. I remembered the bread. I do hope Mrs M. bought the fish. I left her a note.

Babs I really couldn't say.

Peggy Are you in tonight—or not?

Babs Definitely not!

Peggy I was afraid of that. Howard's coming over and we did hope to go out somewhere. It isn't fair to leave Julie alone with the old man. How is he today anyway?

Babs Just the same I gather. He woke me up banging on the floor for attention.

Peggy He's still in good spirits then.

Babs As usual.

Julie enters with the hot-water bottle

Julie Oh, hallo, Peggy, I thought it was you.

Peggy Did Mrs M. leave some fish?

Julie Yes, it's in the fridge.

Peggy That's good. I think I've got everything else.

Babs Give me the hottie. I'll take it in to him, then I'll go up and put the bath on—O.K.?

Peggy Yes, but don't use *all* the hot water, will you?

Babs I'll try not to.

Babs exits to the hall

(*Off*) I don't know why you want a hot-water bottle on a day like this.

Grandad (*off*) I'm bloody cold, that's why. It's all very well for you young 'uns . . .

Peggy (*resting her shopping-bag on an armchair*) Really, the old man is as stubborn as a mule. He should be in hospital where he can be looked after properly.

Julie He always says he wants to die in his own bed.

Peggy That's all very well, but how are we supposed to cope? It's different for Babs, she's used to sick people, but I'm not and frankly some of the jobs we have to do for him I find really distasteful.

Julie So do I. The other evening when I took his supper in, he took his teeth out and told me to clean them for him. I was very nearly sick on the spot.

Peggy That's just like him. Nobody knows what we have to put up with— what we've had to put up with for years. Howard knows, of course, he understands, but he keeps on telling me it can't go on for ever, the old boy's eighty-eight now. But I say to him, how long is for ever? We're not getting any younger, and sometimes I think we'll never be able to get married at this rate.

Julie I don't know why you just don't go ahead and get married. You can't wait for ever.

Peggy I promised Mother I'd look after her father as long as he lived, didn't I? I just didn't expect him to live so long, that's all.

Babs enters from the hall carrying her curlers in a sponge-bag

Babs Ah, the vultures gather at the graveside!

Peggy (*stiffly*) I don't know what you mean by that, Babs. I'm sure I've done my share of looking after the old man, but quite frankly he's out-lived his usefulness.

Babs So might we all one day—have you ever thought of that?

Peggy I'm sure I shall never be awkward and obstinate like Grandad. I wouldn't be a burden to anyone.

Babs None of us know how we'll be when we're old. You should see some of the cases I've dealt with . . .

Peggy (*interrupting quickly*) I don't want to know, thank you. I've had quite enough of your lurid descriptions before—usually at meal-times, and strange as it may seem I prefer my food ungarnished by your medical memoirs!

Babs (*with a shrug*) Point taken!

The kettle whistles in the kitchen

Peggy I'll make some tea!

Peggy exits to the kitchen with the shopping-bag

Babs God, that girl is so upperty at times!

Julie She doesn't mean it. It's just her way.

Babs She's such a martyr. You'd think that no-one else had to put up with anything but her. I don't know how Howard stands it.

Julie He doesn't live with her. Besides, he's not as critical as you.

Babs Well, she's critical of me. Always sniping away at my behaviour like a crabby old maiden aunt!

Julie She's unhappy.

Babs All right, I know you're doing your utmost to be loyal. I'll drop the subject. It's just a little healthy sibling rivalry, that's all. (*She rises and goes to the fireplace, with her curlers*) I'm going to set my hair while I have a bath, and perhaps you'd comb it out for me.

Julie Yes, of course.

Babs Not that it matters what it looks like. He's only interested in my bones. (*She begins to roll her hair up in curlers*)

Julie Your bones?

Babs Yes, the first time I went out with him he told me I had lovely bones. He is orthopaedic, after all.

Julie I thought men were more interested in flesh than bones.

Babs That too. One thing about doctors, they know how to give a girl a good time. They're so desperately anxious to escape from all that ghastly reality on the wards, I suppose.

Julie (*thoughtfully*) Yes, it must be awful, people ill and dying all the time —I should hate it.

Babs It is awful, but it makes you appreciate all the good things of life I can tell you. Pleasure is a popular pursuit of we medicos, believe it or not!

Julie If *you're* anything to go by, it is. I can't believe all nurses are like you.

Babs No, we've got some pious ones as well, and some like Peggy, po-faced and super-efficient. But the sensible ones are like me—pleasure-seekers. Why not? We work hard and we play hard.

Julie Is that really all life is about?

Babs If you can think of anything else, you tell me. (*Seriously*) Let's face it, we're all victims of our environment. If you don't happen to like it, you have to find a means of escape. Your studying has been a means of escape, believe it or not, but at least it's paid off now. For Peggy and me there isn't any way out, so I escape into work and pleasure and she escapes into work and martyrdom. (*Reflectively, glancing across at Julie*) We're both trapped, doomed, really. Perhaps we always were— with our family background. You're lucky you can't remember it too well.

Julie You don't have to make me feel guilty because I'm getting out.

Babs I don't mean to. Why shouldn't you? You've worked for it. I could no more sit poring over books day and night the way you have than I could—fly over the moon!

Julie I have studied hard, but it hasn't been any effort. I prefer the world inside books to the one outside—(*she waves her hand to take in the room*)—than all this!

Babs Life isn't all bad, duckie! It can be nice, too! (*She gives Julie a knowing wink*)

Julie (*with a sigh*) Oh, I know it can be, but it isn't for us, is it? Not very often. There's always been Grandad. (*She looks towards the door*) I've always been afraid of him. When I was a little girl if I cried he used to tell me he'd lock me in the cellar, and I was so scared of the dark. He was so big and frightening. I don't think he meant the things he said, but I believed him. Now he's old and frail, yet he still frightens me. I've only really worked so hard to get away from *him*.

Babs That's funny! Because he thinks you've worked so hard to please him. He told me so the other day. She's worth ten of you, he said to me,

but he knows I never take him seriously. Yes, I said, nobody would
think she was *your* granddaughter, not with *her* brains! He just laughed.

Peggy enters with four cups of tea on a tray

Peggy That bath water will be coming down the stairs in a minute, Babs,
if you don't make an effort.
Babs Oh yes, I forgot. (*She finishes off her hair quickly*)
Peggy On your way you can take the old man a cup of tea.
Babs Why is it always me?
Peggy You're so good at it!
Babs Thanks very much. I'll take the tray then, if you don't mind.

*Peggy removes two cups of tea and puts them on the table by the armchair,
then hands the tray with the remaining cups of tea to Babs*

I'll take mine upstairs, if you don't mind.

Babs exits to the hall

Peggy sits in the armchair

(*Off*) Here you are, Grandad, a nice cuppa for you.
Grandad (*off*) And about bloody time, too!
Babs (*off*) Oh, come on, you don't mean that. All the best things come to
those who wait.
Peggy (*sourly*) Just listen to her buttering him up. I don't know what she
thinks she's going to get out of it.
Julie I don't think it's like that, Peg. I think she really likes him.
Peggy I'm blowed if I do—the old ogre! He's hung over this house like
a malignant presence for as long as I can remember. If only I hadn't
made that promise to Mother I assure you I'd have found an Old
People's Home for him long ago—money or no money!
Julie (*lightly*) Wouldn't it be funny if there wasn't any money at all! If
he'd just been having us on!
Peggy Oh, don't say that. All this agony for nothing. Good God, we
surely deserve some recompense for looking after him all these years?
No, he must have money, I'm convinced of it. We were talking about it
the other day, Howard and I, making a few plans. We've waited such a
long time to get married, we deserve a little help to give us a good
start.
Julie It doesn't seem right, somehow, just waiting for him to die to get
our hands on his money.
Peggy Why ever not? We're entitled to it, aren't we? Look, what we've
had to give up for him . . .
Julie He can't help being ill.
Peggy Oh, long before he was ill. He's always been overbearing and difficult to live with. He's ruined our social life for years. We daren't bring
anyone home in case he was rude to them.

Julie Yes, that's right. Any poor boyfriend who ever plucked up the courage to call on us was greeted with the same remark—"Who the bloody hell are you?" It was only the brave ones who ever survived meeting Grandad!

Peggy Fortunately Howard managed it. I don't know why.

Julie Sheer perseverance.

Peggy Yes, he has plenty of that. (*She rises and begins to lay the table, fetching the cloth and cutlery from the sideboard*)

Julie Still, perhaps the old man was only trying to protect us in his own funny way.

Peggy I'd like to agree with you but I don't believe it's so. I think he's just like an old stag who would fight anyone who threatened his territory. We're here and here we'll stay as long as he can hopefully keep us to dance attendance on him. And we're much too civilized to push him out of the way.

Julie How could we?

Peggy (*thoughtfully*) I don't know, but there ought to be a way. I suppose his fish must be ready by now. It's smelling the house out.

She goes off into the kitchen, talking as she does so

(*Off*) Yes, it's nicely poached. I expect he'll moan but the doctor says he must stick to a light diet, no matter what he wants. I've got the tray ready . . .

She re-enters with a covered dish on a tray, salt and pepper and bread and butter

It's no good, he simply can't have meat pudding and jam roly-poly whatever he says.

Julie I imagine if you get to his age you feel you should be able to eat what you like.

Peggy The doctor said not. You be a dear and take it in to him.

Julie Oh, must I?

Peggy Tell him I'm opening a tin of rice pudding, that should cheer him up.

Julie Oh, all right. I suppose I'll have to help him with it. I just hope he doesn't take his teeth out—that's all.

Julie goes off to the hall

There is a knock at the door

Peggy I'll see to it. It might be Howard.

Peggy goes off to the front door, and returns with Mrs Moore

Mrs Moore Sorry to bother you, dear—I forgot my key.

Peggy It's no bother.

Mrs Moore It just occurred to me when I got home, but I couldn't come back right away because of my Charlie's dinner, so I thought I'd just get on with it, tripe and onions, his favourite, and then while it was cooking I'd come back. I thought it might be important . . .

Peggy What?

Mrs Moore This morning. The old man decided to write out another Will.

Peggy Another Will?

Mrs Moore Yes, he sent me out specially to get one of those forms, and I propped him up on his pillow with a big tray to rest on and he wrote it out. It took him a while, him being so weak, but he managed it, and at the end he asked me and the doctor to witness his signature. I suppose it's all legal, I don't know, but I thought I'd better tell you about it any way.

Peggy Yes, quite right.

Mrs Moore 'Course, I don't know what's in it, like. I just signed me name at the bottom under his.

Peggy What did he do with it afterwards? I mean, where is it now?

Mrs Moore That's what I came to tell you. He said to me to stick it away in his top drawer, you know, his secret drawer as he calls it with the lock, but I clean forgot and I just stuck it on the mantelpiece next to his new pills. Somehow it went out of me head afterwards, I don't know why, I was busy I suppose. That's why I came to tell you. It's in a buff envelope. You can put it away for him, duck, can't you?

Peggy Oh yes, of course.

Mrs Moore Beats me why he wants to make a Will, really, with you three girls his only relatives, but my Charlie says it's much easier if there's a Will, saves time and that.

Peggy Yes, but he's already made his Will—two years ago.

Mrs Moore Oh, that's funny, isn't it? Well, it's none of my business, I'm sure. Old people are like that sometimes with their money. Keep making Wills and all that. Gives them something to think about, I suppose. Still, I 'ope he hasn't gone and left all his money to a Cat's 'ome, not after all you've done for him, anyway.

Peggy I certainly hope not.

Mrs Moore I must be going—oh, there was the other thing, the new pills, did Julie tell you?

Peggy No, what about them?

Mrs Moore The doctor left him some new pills in case he has another attack. He's to take one right away the doctor says, it's a matter of life and death, he said, and to be sure and tell you.

Peggy Oh, thank you. What did the doctor think about him?

Mrs Moore Well, he said to me, the way you girls look after him he could live to be a hundred! Must go now—toodle-oo! I'll see myself out.

Mrs Moore exits to the hall and front door

Peggy (*miserably*) Live to be a hundred—oh no!

Babs enters, her hair in curlers, wearing a cocktail dress and carrying her coat

Babs Who was that?

Peggy Mrs M.

Babs What did she want? (*Putting the coat over a chair*)

Peggy Oh, just something about the shopping tomorrow, nothing important. Have you had a bath already?

Babs A quick splosh. (*She begins to make up her face and do her hair in front of the mirror*)

Peggy You're not going to wear that dress, are you?

Babs Why not? I like it.

Peggy It's too low.

Babs That's why I like it.

Peggy Oh, really, Babs . . .

Babs Where's Julie?

Peggy Giving Grandad his tea, since you weren't here.

Babs Oh, sorry, was it my turn?

Peggy You know she doesn't like going in there.

Babs It's the smell of death. Nobody likes it.

Peggy At least you're used to it.

Babs I do my share, don't I?

Peggy You're always going out. It isn't fair to leave Julie on her own. She gets scared in case something happens.

Babs There's nothing to be scared about. The dead can't hurt you.

Peggy It's finding him. She's scared of finding him like that!

Babs She needn't worry. He's good for another ten years at least.

Peggy Apparently that's what the doctor said. I thought you couldn't keep having strokes and surviving.

Babs He's only had one. You usually don't survive three. In any case, with all the modern medicines we've got nowadays it's possible to keep someone going for years.

Peggy Oh God, I don't know whether I can stand much more! Howard was saying the other night that we ought to get married soon.

Babs So you should.

Peggy How can we—with *him* in there?

Babs Why not? Howard could come and live here.

Peggy Oh no! I can't think of anything worse. That's not the way I want it to be.

Babs We can't always have what we want!

Peggy (*grimly*) Don't I know it!

Babs How you two can keep your passion on ice for years I really don't know! How long have you been engaged now—two years isn't it?

Peggy Yes—almost.

Babs Well, then!

Peggy Well, then, what? There's nothing I can do about it.

Babs You must be about as sexy as a couple of dead fish!

Peggy I'm talking about marriage, not sex!

Babs Oh, silly me! I always thought there was some connection. (*Fuming over her hair*) Damn it, my hair won't go right tonight.

Peggy It isn't just sex. I'm not like *you*. What I want is a home of my own, and children before I'm too old to enjoy them.

Babs You are laying it on thick, you poor thing. Wait a mo' and I'll fetch my violin!

Peggy (*crossly*) You don't understand, do you? You're so flippant. I've had to make sacrifices all my life for you and Julie and I'm sick of it. I want something for myself.

Babs Then grab it!

Peggy Just like that!

Babs Of course. If you know what you want go after it, like I do—as long as you are quite sure it is what you want. (*She stands back from the mirror*) Will I do?

Peggy (*tartly*) Oh, very glamorous!

Babs I'm off then. (*She takes her coat off the chair*) I don't know when I'll be back.

Peggy Tomorrow morning?

Babs (*with a cheerful shrug*) It's possible! (*She gives Peggy an amused wink*)

Babs goes off to the hall and front door, which slams

Left alone, Peggy sighs, presses her hands on her face and shows signs of strain

Julie enters with the tray

Julie (*looking round*) Has Babs gone? I was going to do her hair.

Peggy (*absently*) She did it herself. It looked all right. (*Looking at the tray*) He ate everything then?

Julie Yes, and he kept his teeth in. He doesn't want anything else though.

Peggy I'll take the tray. (*She takes the tray from her, and is about to go off into the kitchen*)

Julie Peggy . . .

Peggy Yes?

Julie Look what he gave me—the old boy! (*She holds out four five-pound notes*)

Peggy (*gasping*) Well—what on earth for?

Julie I don't know. He just told me to take it and go out and have a good time. Isn't it funny? He's never done anything like that before.

Peggy (*ruefully*) You are the blue-eyed girl today!

Julie (*happily*) Yes. I'm so pleased. I'd worked out my budget, and it was a bit tight. Now I'll even have some to spare. What shall I do with it?

Peggy Save it. You never know . . .

Julie No, I just can't save it all. I must do what he says and spend some. I've had such a boring time for so long—books, and studying, and working in a café, no, I'll jolly well spend it, or some of it at any rate. I'll go round to Christine's and ask her to come out with me. We'll go to a disco or something. Oh, I wish he'd given it to me earlier so that I could have bought something new to wear.

Peggy You're just like Babs—money burns a hole in your pocket.

Julie Oh, you don't blame me—do you? It's not as if I've ever been allowed to be extravagant.

Peggy No, go on—you go out. (*She turns away again with the tray*)

Julie Oh—did you want to go out? I didn't think of that.

Peggy No, no, it doesn't matter. Off you go!

Peggy exits to the kitchen

Julie looks after her doubtfully for a minute, then looks back at the money in her hand with a little smile

Julie goes off to the hall. Peggy enters, opens the hall door, listens for a moment, then goes off, leaving the door open. She returns very shortly carrying a buff envelope and a jar of pills. She puts the jar down on the sideboard and, taking the Will out of the envelope, starts to read it. She is obviously shaken by what she reads, and has to sit down

There is a knock at the front door. Peggy starts, rises, puts the Will back into the envelope and puts the envelope into her handbag on the sideboard

Peggy exits to the hall

Peggy (*off*) I thought it must be you.

Howard (*off*) I came straight from work.

Peggy enters, followed by Howard. He is Peggy's fiancé, aged thirty-five, a pleasant, amiable artisan—not as conventional as Peggy and at times irritated by her gentility. He is inclined to be facetious, and is a good mixer

Peggy Been working late?

Howard Just balancing the books. You can't work set hours in your own business, love.

Peggy No, of course not. (*She kisses him solicitously*) Are you tired?

Howard Not too bad. I've got enough energy to take you out somewhere if that's what you'd like.

Peggy I would like, but it isn't possible, I'm afraid. Babs is out on the town and I just told Julie she could go out as well. I didn't think you'd mind.

Howard (*shortly*) No—of course I don't mind. We can always play cards or watch television.

Peggy I'm sorry, but someone has got to stay in.

Howard Oh, all right. I'll slip round to the off-licence and get some booze. That might cheer things up a bit.

Peggy Yes, all right. And I'll make something to eat. At least we'll be together.

Howard Yes, of course. (*He is about to go off when Peggy calls him back*)

Peggy Howard . . .

Howard Yes?

Peggy I wanted to ask you something—about Wills. I mean is a Will legal if it's just written on one of those forms you buy, without being drawn up properly by a solicitor?

Howard Of course it's legal, as long as the signature is witnessed. You can write your last Will and Testament on the back of an envelope if you want to—it's perfectly legal. Why do you ask?

Peggy Oh nothing . . .

Howard Something to do with the old man?

Peggy It's just that Mrs Moore said something about him wanting to make another Will, and I knew he'd already made one because you witnessed it, didn't you?

Howard Yes—about two years ago now. He made me an executor. It must be around somewhere. He swore he'd never spend money on solicitor's fees.

Peggy But if he made another one, a later one, the first one would be cancelled out?

Howard Null and void, that's it.

Peggy (*thoughtfully*) I see.

Howard But why should he make another Will? He hasn't anyone else to leave the money to but you girls.

Peggy I know, but supposing he decided to leave it to just one of us?

Howard He wouldn't do that. Would he?

Peggy (*after a pause*) I don't know. He's so cranky and awkward at times . . .

Howard But it wouldn't be reasonable. He told me there'd be about fifteen thousand pounds apiece. Why should he decide to give it to just one of you?

Peggy I'm not saying he has. I just thought it was possible.

Howard It isn't even remotely possible.

Peggy You know the way he reveres education, never having had any himself. He might think Julie could do with it all to help her with her career.

Howard (*dismissing it*) No, no, he wouldn't do that. It wouldn't be fair.

Peggy Just as if he'd care. He's just given her twenty pounds for no apparent reason—that's far more than he's ever given me.

Howard (*relieved*) Oh, is that all that's wrong with you? I wondered what had put the idea in your head. Just because he feels like spoiling her a bit—why not? She's the youngest, and she's done well at school. That doesn't mean he'd leave her all his money.

Peggy (*with a sigh*) Would it really make so much difference if he did?

Howard What do you mean?

Peggy To us?

Howard (*hesitantly*) It must make some difference, Peg, of course. I'm

having a hard struggle at the moment with the business. I couldn't begin
to take out a mortgage as well.

Peggy (*with a rueful smile*) I see. Thank you for being so honest.

Howard (*going over to her*) Don't get me wrong, darling. I wouldn't let
you down. We'd just have to wait a bit longer, that's all.

Peggy (*gloomily*) That's all! (*Looking at Howard thoughtfully*) If only one
could make time stand still. Perhaps a few years don't matter much to
a man, but to a woman it's different. I can feel the sands of time run-
ning out . . .

Howard Oh God, we're not drawing our old age pensions yet.

Peggy (*exasperated with his inability to understand*) *I'm* getting older,
Howard, every day . . .

Howard (*puzzled*) We all are.

Julie enters from the hall, having changed her clothes

Julie Oh hallo, Howard. Did Peggy tell you about my good luck?

Howard (*putting his arm round her*) Yes—aren't you the lucky one?
What ever came over the old basket?

Julie I dunno I'm sure, but I'm glad it happened when I was in the
vicinity.

Howard It's better to be lucky than clever, they say, and you're both.

Julie (*pleased*) I suppose I am. Oh, that sounds very big-headed.

Howard Nonsense! You must have confidence in yourself. Most people
take you at your own valuation, you know.

Julie Do they?

Howard That's my experience, anyway.

Julie I'm just dying to go round and tell my friend about this. You don't
mind too much, do you? Peggy said it would be all right . . .

Howard (*valiantly*) No, of course not.

Peggy I've already told you . . .

Howard I'll give you a lift if you like. I'm just going round to the off-
licence.

Julie Oh, thanks, that's nice of you. (*Looking across doubtfully at Peggy*)
If you're sure you don't mind . . .

Peggy (*irritably*) I've said so—haven't I?

Howard (*as they go off*) Won't be long.

Peggy All right. Don't be late, Julie . . .

Julie No, of course not. 'Bye, then.

Julie and Howard exit through the hall, and the front door slams

*Peggy waits until she hears the car drive off, then takes the Will out of her
handbag and reads it again. This time she looks really angry. She begins to
walk up and down the room in agitation. The banging begins off—a very
urgent banging. Instinctively Peggy moves towards the hall door. She puts
the Will on the sideboard*

Peggy All right, all right, I'm coming.

Peggy exits to the hall, but returns almost at once

The banging continues, but weaker

The pills—the pills . . . (*She picks up the pills from the sideboard and is going back to the door when a thought occurs to her, and she stops and looks at them. Then with great deliberation she takes them over to the mantelpiece and drops them behind the fireguard. Then she goes back for the Will and picks it up. Carefully she shuts the door*)

The banging becomes weaker still. Peggy takes the Will to a metal waste-paper-basket by the fireplace, takes some matches from the mantelpiece, and starts to burn it. The banging subsides as—

the CURTAIN *falls*

SCENE 2

The same. Morning, two weeks later

As the CURTAIN *rises Mr Dalrymple is discovered in a wheel-chair with a rug over his knees, dozing. The wheel chair takes the place of the main armchair, which has been pushed against the wall by the fireplace. Mr Dalrymple, the grandfather, is aged eighty-eight. Though he has suffered a stroke and does not speak at all when he is in the room his expression conveys that he is well aware of what is going on. He is a cunning old man, tenacious to the end*

Julian Fudge enters from the hall with some pills and a small glass of water on a tray. He is wearing a white coat over his indoor clothes. Julian is in his late twenties, a bit "woopsie" but with a sense of humour and lots of personality. He works as a male nurse; a smart young man with an ingratiating manner, ambitious and with an eye to the main chance

Julian Here we are, duckie, just what the doctor ordered. (*He puts the tray down on the sideboard and fusses around the old man, tucking in the rug, etc.*) You look as snug as a bug in a rug, Mr Dalrymple. You just take your medicine like a good boy and you can have a little rest. (*He brings the pills and water over and gives the old man one of them*) Down the hatch now—that's good!

Mr Dalrymple swallows a pill with some difficulty

Mrs Moore enters from the kitchen

Mrs Moore Oh, Mr Fudge, I thought I heard your voice. I was only saying to Peggy yesterday what a good job you're doing with the old man. Who'd 'ave thought it, him sitting up in a chair as large as life and twice as natural! Only a week ago we thought he was a gonner.

Julian Oh, he's very resilient is Grandpop! (*He pats him on the head affectionately*) Mind you, he did have a nasty turn.

Mrs Moore He did that! He must have been bad to let them cart him off to hospital. Hates institutions he does. Still, he wasn't in long. Soon as he was able to sit up he discharged himself.

Julian A man of character, that's what he is!

Mrs Moore Gave the girls a nasty shock I can tell you!

Julian I'm sure it did. Thought you were on your way out, Pop, did they? But you showed them.

Mr Dalrymple nods appreciatively

Mrs Moore (*in a hoarse whisper*) Can he understand?

Julian Of course he can. He's not barmy just because he's lost his power of speech. He knows everything that's going on, believe me.

Mrs Moore Doesn't seem right, though, does it, just sitting there, like that, not able to do nothing for himself. I 'ope I get took before I end up like that. Still, I suppose I shouldn't say that. We all 'ave to go in God's good time, don't we?

Julian Some of the old folk I've looked after they've begged me for an overdose—you'd never believe it. I couldn't oblige them, of course, it's more than my job's worth.

Mrs Moore (*admiringly*) Dedicated—that's what you are. It must be such a relief to them girls, having a professional to look after the old boy.

Julian I aim to please!

Mrs Moore If only you'd been here when he was took bad I daresay it wouldn't have happened at all. He had some new pills, you see, prescribed that very day just for that sort of emergency but the girls couldn't find them—funny thing that.

Julian (*with interest*) Yes, isn't it?

Mrs Moore 'Course when I told my Charlie, he said he wasn't at all surprised the old boy was took bad that day because he'd just made a new Will, and that seemed like a bad omen, somehow, making a new Will.

Julian (*thoughtfully*) Mm—yes, it's an interesting point of view. Worth a few bob, the old boy, is he?

Mrs Moore I should say! (*Shouting*) Looked after number one, haven't you, Mr Dalrymple? So you should! Nobody else will.

Mr Dalrymple nods in agreement

Not that it will do him much good now, will it? Make the most of life while you can, that's what I say. None of us know how we'll end up. If we did, perhaps we wouldn't wait. Oh, well, I must get on. Like some coffee, would you?

Julian No thanks. I'm going to take the old boy out for a walk. It's such a nice day. It will do him good.

Mrs Moore Right you are then. See you later.

Mrs Moore goes off to the kitchen

Julian You'd like that, wouldn't you, Mr Dalrymple? (*He shouts*) A little walk, eh? A short perambulation?

Julian moves away, and Mr Dalrymple reaches out and plucks at his sleeve

What is it? Something you want?

Mr Dalrymple makes a movement with his hand as if writing

(*Nodding agreeably*) Yes, yes, I understand. We'll see to that little matter. Don't worry. I'll just get your coat. (*He goes towards the hall*)

Babs enters from the hall, in her dressing-gown

Babs Oh, hallo—I'd forgotten you'd be here. I hope you'll excuse my attire.

Julian Don't mind me! I'm like one of the family when I'm looking after somebody. At least, I try to be. I was just thinking of taking the old boy out for a walk.

Babs Yes, why not? A change of scenery would do him good. How are you today, Grandad, O.K.?

Mr Dalrymple nods

He looks better than I do. Oh, my head—it feels as if it isn't quite on my shoulders. (*She sits*)

Julian Tut, tut! You naughty girl! Out on the tiles, were you?

Babs You could say that.

Julian Over-imbibing and all that?

Babs A bit, but I like it, you see, at the time.

Julian Don't we all?

Babs I'm on duty tonight as well. I don't know how I'll get through the night. About half-past three in the morning, that's when I begin to flag.

Julian The human body is at its lowest ebb then, didn't you know? That's when most people die.

Babs Yes, we do seem to have a lot of deaths around that time. Did you do much night duty?

Julian No more than I could help. It interfered with my social life.

Babs Yes, it does that! You prefer private nursing, do you?

Julian Oh much. You get to know the patients, and there's much more freedom. Take Grandpop here, he isn't much trouble at all. Strictly speaking, I wouldn't say I was necessary, but Dr Marshall wanted someone here. It was unfortunate, you see, when he had his last stroke that there was no-one here to give him his pills.

Babs Oh, Peggy was here. But she couldn't find them.

Julian Funny that—that she couldn't find them.

Babs She lost her head. She isn't trained—like you and me.

Julian No, but still . . . (*He is thoughtful for a moment*) I wouldn't have thought she was the type—to lose her head, would you?

Babs Not really. But I've seen some very cool customers go to pieces in an emergency. I'm sure you have as well,

Julian I suppose I have—at some time or other.
Babs I think I'll make some coffee. Would you like a cup?
Julian No thanks. I was just about to take the old boy for a walk when you came in. I'll just get his coat.

Julian goes into the hall

Babs (*shouting*) That will be nice for you, Grandad! Going out in the fresh air!

Julian returns with Mr Dalrymple's coat and hat

Julian I have to go to the shop anyway. Something he wants.
Babs (*helping him put the coat on Mr Dalrymple*) Beats me how you manage to communicate with him. How do you know he wants something?
Julian Oh, we communicate all right. Little nods and winks, and a bit of sign language. Besides, he can write a bit if I guide his hand.
Babs (*surprised*) I didn't realize that.
Julian There's plenty of life in the old dog yet. There we are. Come on, now, me old love.

Julian takes Mr Dalrymple in his chair off to the hall, meeting Julie there. Babs goes into the kitchen

Julie (*off*) Oh hallo—going out?
Julian (*off*) Yes, we're going for a little constitutional.
Julie (*off*) Is he all right?
Julian (*off*) Of course. It will do him good. Toodlepip!

The front door slams

Julie enters, looking rather disconsolate. Babs comes back from the kitchen

Babs The coffee's percolating. Do you want some?
Julie No thanks.
Babs (*calling out*) Just for me thanks, Mrs M. Black!
Mrs Moore (*off*) All right, dear. I'll see to it.
Babs Oh God, my head! (*She sits down again*) Why did I move?
Julie Heavy night, was it?
Babs Uh-huh! (*She holds her aching temples*)
Julie Swami again?
Babs Yes. It's getting to be a habit, isn't it? I shall have to stop seeing him soon or he'll start getting possessive. Oh, I do wish I'd refused that last glass of wine. (*She shuts her eyes and leans back in the chair*)
Julie (*hesitantly*) Babs, I've got something to tell you.
Babs (*alarmed*) What's that? You sound nervous somehow. Not man trouble, I hope.

Julie Not as far as I'm concerned.

Babs That's a relief. For a moment, I thought—there goes my little sister's career down the drain! I suppose it's my dirty mind, thinking all trouble must have something to do with a man.

Julie Well, it has something to do with a man.

Babs The Chef didn't rape you over the deep-freeze, I suppose?

Julie Don't be silly!

Babs Go on, then—spit it out!

Julie (*with an effort*) You know I don't usually go into the café on a Saturday morning, only this week they asked me particularly because the other girl's off sick. They want me to go in tonight as well . . .

Babs So—what happened? Something must have happened this morning, I suppose, for you to be so mysterious.

Julie Somebody came in for coffee—you'll never guess who.

Babs Let me try. Omar Sharif!

Julie Of course not.

Babs I thought it was too much to hope for. Well, who then?

Julie Howard.

Babs I see. Howard. So what? Even dear old Howard is entitled to a coffee break from all that hard work he does, isn't he?

Julie But he wasn't alone.

Babs Ah, the plot thickens!

Julie Oh, do stop assing about. He was with a woman, a blonde, rather pretty in an obvious sort of way, lots of eye make-up, you know the type.

Babs Like me?

Julie No, not like you. Much older.

Babs Perhaps it was his mother.

Julie It wasn't his mother. I've met Howard's mother. Oh, Babs, I wish you'd be serious for a minute.

Babs All right, I'll try! So Howard was drinking coffee in your café with a rather pretty older woman. I still say so what?

Julie It was the way they were behaving, sort of lovie-dovie. You know what I mean, holding hands across the table, and gazing into one another's eyes, and sort of laughing at nothing. I've never seen him behave like that with Peg.

Babs (*seriously now*) Neither have I.

Julie What do you make of it?

Babs I don't know. It could be just a flirtation. Did he see you?

Julie No, he obviously didn't think I worked on a Saturday morning, or he wouldn't have taken her in there. I don't think he saw me, because as soon as I realized it was him I hid in the kitchen until he'd gone. The boss was getting quite cross with me.

Babs It doesn't sound like Howard, does it? It's a bit reckless, really. Perhaps there's more to him than I realized.

Julie You sound as if you admired him. Well, I certainly don't. Peggy would be so hurt if she knew. How could he behave like that, in the same town where everybody knows he's engaged to Peggy? It's really unkind!

Babs Perhaps he's got tired of playing footsie-wootsie with Peg. I did warn her this might happen.

Julie You warned her?

Babs (*with a shrug*) She's been keeping him at arm's length for too long. I told her as much. It's all very well playing hard to get, but if you're too hard you run the risk of not being wanted after all, like the fox and the grapes. Perhaps Howard has decided it's not worth waiting for.

Julie That doesn't say much for him then, the beast!

Babs Don't be so intolerant, duckie! Live and let live. A little girl like you can't possibly imagine what it's like having to cope with great big mature emotions. You shouldn't be so anxious to judge him.

Julie It will make Peggy so unhappy, and she's already in a state of nerves with all the worry over Grandad.

Babs I wonder whether we ought to tell her.

Julie Oh no—I only told you because I couldn't bear to keep it to myself.

Babs Yes, but if we did tell her, it might make her come to her senses. Besides, if they're that open about it, somebody else is bound to find out, and it's surely better for her to hear it from her own sisters than some interfering stranger.

Julie I don't know. I wish I hadn't mentioned it now.

Babs I'll tell her, don't worry. I'll break it gently.

Mrs Moore enters with coffee in a jug, and cream, together with three cups

Mrs Moore Here you are, my dears. I've put a cup on there for Peggy, she won't be long. And you can have it nice and black, Babs. It will do you good—plenty of sugar, too. My Charlie says you need plenty of sugar when you've got a hangover.

Babs Yes, but I can't bear sugar. I like coffee strong and black, just the way I like my men!

Mrs Moore (*with a cackle of laughter*) Ooh, you are a one! I'll tell my Charlie that. He'll have a laugh! I must be going in a minute. I've done the veg. I must say I like having that nice Mr Fudge about the house, don't you? Nice person he is, so gay!

Babs I had that impression, too!

Mrs Moore Nice and cheerful. I like cheerful people. Like my Charlie, always cracking jokes. He'll be cracking jokes on his death-bed, will my Charlie. But the old boy looks better for having a man looking after him, doesn't he? He was too much for you girls!

Babs Yes, it was good of Dr Marshall to arrange it. And it isn't costing us a penny. All on the taxpayers.

Mrs Moore Well, why not? That's what it's there for, isn't it? I'm not proud, not me. Minute I'm out of work down I go to draw my dole, only they don't call it that now, but whatever it is I reckon I'm entitled to it. It's no good having a Welfare State if you don't benefit from it, is it, that's what my Charlie always says.

Babs I'm actually beginning to feel quite normal. This coffee is very good!

Mrs Moore What you need is a hair of the dog. The pubs are open. Why
don't you go down and 'ave one?

Babs Oh no, I'm much too shy to go into a pub on my own!

Mrs Moore You shy! (*She laughs*) That'll be the day! I'm going now, then.
See you Monday. Cheeribye!

Julie 'Bye!

Babs 'Bye!

Mrs Moore exits through the hall and the door slams

Julie Oh dear, I feel so wretched. Poor Peggy! Why do we have to have
so much trouble in our family? Other people don't.

Babs How do you know what suffering goes on behind drawn blinds?
Everybody has troubles. We're not exceptional.

Julie We seem to have more than other people.

Babs We've had our fair share, but it's all cause and effect. It all goes
back to the old man, really, the sort of person he is, ruling us all with a
rod of iron when we were kids, and our own father being such a useless
individual. It's a curse—unhappy parents have unhappy children, and so
it goes on—like an interminable treadwheel. It's very hard to get off!

Julie You make me frightened when you talk like that. A curse on us!
Why, there's no hope for us then?

Babs *You* can break it. *I've told you.* You're the only one who can.

*Peggy enters with a shopping-bag full of shopping. She tries hard to be
bright and breezy but she is obviously in a state of nervous tension and
very unhappy*

Peggy Oh hallo, you two! I think I've got everything. The shops were full
as usual on a Saturday. I really hate the week-end shopping. It would be
nice sometimes if my sisters took a turn to do it.

Julie (*quickly*) I had to work this morning.

Peggy Oh yes, I forgot. Your last day, isn't it?

Julie I'm going in this evening. They've got a private party, and then I'm
finished. Praise be!

Peggy You haven't liked it much, have you? Still, it's given you a bit of
pocket money.

Julie I shall need it.

Peggy And next week you leave us. We will miss you, won't we, Babs?

Babs I'll say we will.

Julie No, you won't. Besides, I shall be home again at Christmas.

Peggy Christmas! That seems like a hundred years away! Anything could
have happened by then.

Babs That's more than likely!

Peggy You've got some coffee there, that's good! I'll just plonk these in
the kitchen.

She goes off into the kitchen, still talking

(*Off*) We're having rissoles today, like it or not! (*She leaves the bag in the kitchen*)
Babs Don't mention food, please!
Julie I'm not hungry, either.

Peggy returns

Peggy (*helping herself to some coffee*) Under the weather, are you, Babs?
Babs Just slightly.
Peggy You will do these things!
Babs I enjoyed it at the time. I'm not complaining.
Peggy It sounded to me as if you were complaining. I don't know why you do it—it's ridiculous!
Babs No lectures, please! It was all worth it.
Peggy I'm glad you think so. (*She sits down, kicks off her shoes and lights a cigarette*) God, but my feet ache! Jostling shoppers everywhere. Sometimes I wish we lived in the country, away from it all.
Babs There's nothing to stop you—you and Howard. That is, once the old man . . .
Peggy Oh, don't even mention it. The old man isn't going to die. I'm convinced of it. He'll outlive me, just as he outlived our mother. He'll probably outlive all of us!
Babs That's not very likely.
Peggy The way I feel today it's very likely!

Pause. Babs and Julie exchange glances

Babs (*bluntly*) Julie saw Howard today . . .
Julie No, don't . . .
Peggy So—she saw Howard! Is that so extraordinary in a town of this size?
Babs He was in the café this morning, and he wasn't alone.
Peggy Good! What on earth are you being so ominous about?
Babs He was with another woman.
Peggy He isn't a monk. He can be seen with other women occasionally, you know.
Julie I thought you were going to break it gently.
Babs I'm trying to.
Peggy What is all this? What are you trying to say? (*She looks from one to the other*)
Babs It's just that they were—well, holding hands and all that.
Peggy (*stiffly*) Julie saw this?
Julie Yes, I'm afraid so. They were behaving sort of romantically together.
Babs Mooning over one another.
Peggy (*with a false, harsh laugh*) Don't be absurd! Howard isn't the mooning type. He's never mooned over me.
Babs Exactly.
Peggy What do you mean by that remark?
Babs Just, exactly. He doesn't behave like that with you at all, does he? Either in public or in private.

Peggy (*after a pause, glaring hard at Babs*) I can see you're in one of your irritating moods. Perhaps I'd better get on with the dinner. As usual everything is left to me. (*She stands up, viciously stubbing out her cigarette in the ashtray on the mantelpiece*) You might as well know I'm not a bit interested in your innuendos. I'm quite sure Howard will have a perfectly good explanation for anything you might consider suspicious. (*Angrily, turning on Babs*) The trouble with you, Babs, you're sex-obsessed. You think everybody is like you—but they're not. Howard and I, *we're* not . . . whatever you think, whatever you say . . .

Peggy exits quickly to the kitchen, shutting the door behind her

Julie (*accusingly*) You weren't very tactful. You've hurt her feelings. Oh dear, I wish I'd never told you!
Babs It's her own fault. I've given her enough good advice but she won't take it. She's made her bed, but she won't lie on it!
Julie I wish you wouldn't make fun of people.
Babs I'm not. I'm very sorry for my elder sister, I can tell you. She's going round the twist with sexual frustration, but she doesn't realize it. You can't blame old Howard for straying, the way she treats him! Anyway, if he's got a roving eye it's better for her to find out now than after they're married.
Julie If you don't blame him, I do. I think he's a pig! The way he was looking at that other woman. Oh—it just made me feel ashamed!
Babs That bad, was it? I didn't think he had it in him!
Julie Why are you so—so cynical?
Babs I'm not cynical. I'm realistic. You stick to your dewy-eyed ideals if you want to, my dear, but life really isn't like that. You can't treat a man as if he's stepped out of the pages of a woman's magazine. Men aren't like that. She's been keeping Howard on ice for too long. Something was bound to happen.
Julie He could, at least, have been more discreet!
Babs That's a fact! (*She rises*) I really think I must make an effort, slopping around all day. I'm getting to be a real slut! (*Groaning*) Oh my head. I moved a bit too quickly then. (*She goes slowly over to the hall door*) Perhaps I'll soak in the bath until lunch. It might make me feel like a new woman.
Julie As long as it doesn't make you feel like a new man!
Babs Oh, cheeky, aren't we? Real Cambridge exam stuff that was! (*She hesitates in the doorway*) Oh hell, those stairs look like Mount Everest. Here goes . . .

Babs exits to the hall

Julie (*calling out*) Can I help you, Peg? (*She moves over towards the kitchen*)
Peggy (*off*) No, it's all right. I can manage.

There is a noise in the hall, and Julian appears pushing Mr Dalrymple

Julian (*outside the door*) There we are! That's put roses into your cheeks, that little walk, Grandpop!

Julie Oh—did he enjoy it?

Julian Certainly, why not? Did him the world of good, didn't it, Grandpop? I'll just take him in his room and set him up for his lunch—would you tell your sister?

Julian disappears from sight

Julie Yes, all right. (*She calls out*) Peggy—Mr Fudge is back with Grandad.

Peggy enters

Peggy All right. You'd better go up and change before lunch. That skirt is a bit short and Mr Fudge is staying.

Julie Oh, Babs says I've nothing to fear from him.

Peggy Babs doesn't know everything. Go on . . . (*She crosses to the table and begins to lay it*)

Julie Oh, all right, then . . .

Julie exits, passing Julian, who enters

Julian (*to Peggy*) It's quite tiring, pushing that wheel-chair, you'd be surprised. I feel like Mummy taking the twins for an airing. It's a wonder I didn't have a few old dears coochy-cooing over him!

Peggy It wouldn't surprise me if you did. People are so sentimental, especially in this town.

Julian Yes, I've noticed. (*He shuts the door behind him carefully and watches Peggy as she continues to lay the table, moving between the table and the sideboard*)

Peggy (*after a pause*) The lunch is all on. I'm cooking something light for Grandad.

Julian That's good!

Peggy (*a little embarrassed by his attention, making conversation*) I must say you do get on with him very well.

Julian I've got a way with the old 'uns. It is my trade after all. He talks to me, you know.

Peggy (*alarmed*) Talks to you? But he can't talk . . .

Julian Oh yes, he can—not with his tongue, like other people, but with his hands, with signs and so on. He can write as well, if I guide his hand. I suppose you hadn't realized that.

Peggy (*disturbed*) No—I hadn't.

Julian Like today. He was quite clear about something he wanted me to get him today when we were out. Quite clear about it, he was.

Peggy (*curiously*) Oh?

Julian He's very keen, you know, on making a new Will. Ever so disappointed he was about the other one disappearing.

Peggy (*nervously*) What do you mean—the other one?

Julian Why, the one he made out the day he was taken ill. Surely you remember?

Peggy No—I—I don't think so.

Julian He does. He remembers it all very well. Everything that happened that day.

Peggy (*stopping her chores and listening apprehensively*) Does he?

Julian And he's told me in his own way. We understand each other very well.

Peggy I'm glad . . .

Julian (*with sly enthusiasm*) That's good. I hoped you'd be glad. Because we're going to sit down again this afternoon, the pair of us, and make out the Will all over again, just like the one that disappeared—leaving everything to Julie.

Peggy (*bleakly*) I see.

Julian I thought you might—somehow. See you later.

Julian smiles joylessly, then goes off to the hall

Peggy looks after him fixedly, then turns away and puts her hands over her eyes

Peggy Oh God!

CURTAIN

ACT II

SCENE 1

The same. That evening

The curtains are drawn at the window, and the lights are on. Peggy is standing by the mantelpiece, smoking. She is wearing a simple evening dress. She looks very cross, and glances at her watch impatiently. After a moment Julian taps at the hall door then comes in

Julian Oh, I thought you'd gone out.

Peggy No—my fiancé must have been delayed. He's not usually this late.

Julian Oh, what a shame! Ruined your evening, has it?

Peggy (*stiffly*) Not at all.

Julian There's not much point in me staying on if you're not going out. is there? I mean, it's not really part of my duty to stay in the evening, Not that I mind helping you out, of course, but it does seem a bit pointless both of us being here.

Peggy Yes, of course. You can go if you like.

Julian Thank you. The old boy's been fed and watered, and he's all ready for bed, but he asked me specially if he could see "Match of the Day", and I'm afraid I agreed. I didn't know you'd be in, you see.

Peggy That's all right. I don't care what he sees.

Julian But it's getting him into bed afterwards, isn't it? That's the problem.

Peggy Julie will be back later. She'll help me.

Julian Are you sure?

Peggy Of course, we've managed before. In any case Howard, my fiancé, is bound to turn up sooner or later.

Julian All right then. I'll just go and see if there's anything else he wants before I go. (*He moves to the door*)

Peggy (*impulsively*) Mr Fudge . . .

Julian Yes?

Peggy I was just wondering whether you got round to doing that little job this afternoon.

Julian (*deliberately obtuse*) What was that?

Peggy You said you were going to help Grandad make out a new Will.

Julian Oh yes. No, we didn't manage to do it, after all. He was tired, you see, and anyway we needed the signature of another witness—someone not in the family . . .

Peggy (*relieved*) Oh, I see.

Julian Yes, so we're going to do it on Monday, first thing. I've promised him. He's quite nervous about it for some reason.

Peggy (*crisply*) I can't think why.

Julian He's got some funny little idea that if he doesn't get on with it something will happen to stop him. I can't think why, either, but old people get these funny notions at times.

Peggy Yes, I see. Is that all, then?

Julian Of course. (*He hovers in the doorway*) I was going to tell you we'd postponed writing the Will, actually, but you seemed so upset about it this morning . . .

Peggy (*irritably*) I wasn't in the least upset!

Julian Oh, sorry I'm sure!

Julian goes out, smiling

Left alone, Peggy sits down angrily and begins to read a magazine, turning the pages without really looking at it. There is a knock at the door. She looks up sharply but does not hurry to answer it. She stubs out her cigarette and looks at herself in the mirror first, then she goes to the hall door

Peggy exits

Peggy (*off*) How nice of you to come!

Howard (*off*) I'm sorry I'm late.

Peggy and Howard enter

Peggy Yes, you are a bit. What happened?

Howard I had a rush job on. You know that contract I told you about, up at the old school. We promised to have it finished before the start of term, but we've slipped up. It's the materials, really, we just couldn't get them through in time. Anyway, we had a delivery this afternoon, and I rounded up some men and got them busy right away. I'm really sorry, Peg.

Peggy You might have rung me up. We had a table booked for half-eight, and now it's gone nine.

Howard We can still make it. You're all dressed up. It's a pity not to go out when we have so little opportunity.

Peggy It's too late now. I cancelled the table when you weren't here by nine, and I've just told Mr Fudge he can go home.

Howard Oh hell! You mean we're stuck in again! Where are the others?

Peggy Babs is on duty tonight and Julie is working late at the café. They have a private party or something.

Howard I didn't know she worked on Saturdays.

Peggy She doesn't usually.

Howard (*sighing*) I dashed round here as soon as I could. I only stopped to change. I could do with a pint after the way I've worked today. Can't you ask that male nurse to stay on just for a while?

Peggy I don't see why I should. I was looking forward to an evening out as well, I might say, but I don't mean just half an hour in a smoky pub

so that you can relieve yourself of the day's tensions. I meant a real
evening out—like we used to have. It is a special occasion, after all.

Howard (*puzzled and a little guilty*) Is it?

Peggy You don't remember?

Howard (*racking his brains*) Wait a minute—it'll come to me. It's not your
birthday or my birthday. September, September . . .

Peggy Yes, September! September the twenty-second! The day we got
engaged two years ago!

Howard Oh God! How could I forget that? Honestly, Peggy, I've been so
busy . . .

Peggy Yes, I know how busy you've been. I've heard about it.

Howard What do you mean?

Peggy You're certainly very blasé, aren't you? Taking another woman to
the very café where my sister works!

Howard Oh—oh! This morning!

Peggy Yes, this morning.

Howard It's obvious, isn't it? I wouldn't have gone there if I'd had anything to hide.

Peggy You thought Julie wouldn't be there . . .

Howard I didn't think about it at all. To be honest, I'd forgotten that was
where she worked.

Peggy Now we're getting to the truth.

Howard Don't be unreasonable, Peg, I just took another woman out for
a cup of coffee. She's my secretary, and she came in this morning to
help me out with some invoices so I took her out for a cup of coffee.
Where's the harm in it?

Peggy Your secretary? The one you told me about—the divorcee with two
children?

Howard That's right.

Peggy The pretty blonde one?

Howard She—isn't bad looking.

Peggy Julie said she was pretty, in a very obvious way of course.

Howard She just works for me—I haven't sat down and assessed her looks.

Peggy You were assessing her this morning apparently.

Howard Nonsense!

Peggy Holding hands, and mooning—yes, that's what they told me, mooning over her.

Howard (*trying to laugh it off*) Ridiculous! We may have been flirting a
bit. It didn't mean anything. Just a bit of fun.

Peggy (*sneering*) A bit of fun! I wonder just how far you're prepared to
take your bit of fun!

Howard What do you want me to say?

Peggy The truth.

Howard I doubt that very much. I don't think you want the truth at all.
What you want is a nice comforting little lie.

Peggy You've already told me enough comforting little lies.

Howard (*getting exasperated*) I'm not going to cross my heart and hope
to die, Peg. You believe what you want to believe.

Peggy (*pleadingly*) I want you to reassure me, that's all. Don't you realize what torment it is to think of you with someone else, kissing her, making love to her . . .

Howard I'm hardly likely to make love to her in the middle of The Sunshine Café over a cup of coffee. I'm not that uninhibited!

Peggy You could make the opportunity if you wanted to.

Howard (*unconvincingly*) I don't want to.

Peggy I don't believe you.

Howard (*shrugging*) Please yourself!

Peggy (*bitterly*) All right. If you want to be released . . . (*She tugs at her engagement ring*)

Howard (*going to her*) I don't want to be released. I love you.

Peggy Love on your terms.

Howard Love on flesh and blood terms—yes.

Peggy If only you'd be patient . . .

Howard I've been patient. Good God, the time we've waited we could have had a family by now. We're not getting any younger, either of us. If you want to be sure of me at least make me sure of you.

Peggy What do you mean?

Howard Let's get married right away. Next week, say, or the week after that.

Peggy No, no, I couldn't do that. What would happen to the family?

Howard Let them look after themselves. You've done enough.

Peggy I don't want a rushed wedding. I want to plan it. It only happens once to most people.

Howard We've spent long enough planning and waiting. It's marriage or nothing, Peggy—and soon!

Peggy I can't make a decision just like that!

Howard All right—tomorrow will do.

Peggy Tomorrow!

Howard I'm beginning to wonder if you're not secretly afraid of marriage. All these excuses—perhaps the fact of the matter is that you don't want to commit yourself finally. You just want to keep me stringing along.

Peggy That isn't so! I do want you. I'm not very good at expressing it, but I do, deep down inside. It's just that I want everything to be right—to be perfect.

Howard Nothing is ever perfect. Sometimes I think you expect too much of human beings.

Peggy Perhaps I do. I expect loyalty, that's one thing, and fidelity, and all sorts of old fashioned things like that.

Howard Oh, well, if you're going to start that again I'd better go. We wouldn't enjoy the evening now, the way things are between us.

Peggy I suppose you want to go and see that old blonde? That's it, isn't it? You're going to see her.

Howard If you want to know I'm going to get blind drunk! Good-bye.

Howard storms out, slamming the hall door then the front door

Peggy Oh, damn, damn, damn!

Julian enters silently and stands looking at Peggy

Julian A little altercation, was it? I couldn't help overhearing.

Peggy (*startled*) I thought you'd gone.

Julian No, I was just making the old boy comfy. Besides, I wanted to have a word with you alone, and this seems as good a time as any. Had a lover's tiff, have you? Oh, the stresses and strains of a long engagement! Takes its toll, doesn't it?

Peggy I don't like your tone, Mr Fudge. It's offensive!

Julian Oh, I *am* sorry. I'm sure I don't mean to offend anybody. I'm just naturally interested in people. The families where I go to look after the old folk, I always find myself getting very interested in them. I can't help it really. I don't mean to be a nosey-parker.

Peggy If you have something to say, say it, and then you can go. I'm not in the mood for company tonight.

Julian (*soothingly*) I *do* understand. You poor girl! You've had all the burden and nobody appreciates it, do they? Coming in as an outsider I can see it all, the years you've worked for them, keeping the family together, struggling to see that the young one got her education, and looking after the old boy as well. Oh yes, I can see it all.

Peggy I really don't require your sympathy, Mr Fudge . . .

Julian What I think is that it's time you had your reward. It's all very well to talk about virtue being its own reward, but that doesn't help much, does it? Not when you're in the centre of things, and you see injustice all round you.

Peggy What exactly are you getting at?

Julian That Will. That Will the old man made out the day he had his last stroke—it must have been such a shock to you when you saw what was in it.

Peggy (*taken aback*) Saw what was in it? But I didn't see it. Nobody did. It disappeared—it must have fallen in the fire. He insisted on having a fire in there, even though it wasn't cold. I certainly didn't see what happened to it.

Julian I'd hate to contradict you, Miss Strange, really I would, but you see that isn't the way I understand the story, not at all.

Peggy I don't see how you can possibly know anything about it . . .

Julian You know I'm in the confidence of Mr Dalrymple, don't you? We communicate. I explained that to you before.

Peggy So what?

Julian So he's managed to tell me that he saw you take the Will, you see, off his mantelpiece in there, and his pills too—and you didn't come back with them either, not even when he banged his stick on the floor. In fact, he was so cross about it that's what brought on his stroke. At least that's what I make out of it.

Peggy That's just incredible!

Julian Do you think so? Now to a student of human nature like myself it doesn't sound a bit incredible. You'd be surprised the things that happen in the best of regulated households when an old person with money is on his way out. I've seen so much of it. It has quite a strange effect on some people, the prospect of getting their hands on a bit of extra loot!

Peggy You're really rather insolent, Mr Fudge. I shall have to speak to Dr Marshall about you. You needn't think you're irreplaceable.

Julian I'm your friend, you don't seem to realize that. I understand, really I do. It must have been a very nasty shock when you discovered that he'd decided to leave all his money to young Julie when you're the one who has made the sacrifices.

Peggy How did you know that?

Julian Ah—tripped you up, didn't I? That wasn't the right reply at all. You should have said something like, "He'd never do that", or "You're making it up", not "How did you know that?" That's as good as admitting that *you* knew.

Peggy I didn't, I didn't. Please leave me alone.

Julian Not only did you know about it, but you destroyed the Will in the hope that he'd die before he could make another one. That's it, isn't it? I wouldn't be surprised if you deliberately withheld his pills as well—just to be sure.

Peggy (*in panic*) No, no, stop it, please. I can't take much more.

Julian But he beat you, by getting better, tough old bird that he is! And now he wants his Will made out again. Just the same as before. With all the money going to Julie . . .

Peggy (*softly*) It just isn't fair.

Julian No, it isn't fair, I agree. I told him as much, but he's adamant. These self-made men, they're all the same about education, spend their lives regretting that they didn't have any. Though he's done very well without it, if you ask me! That's not the point. He wants Julie to have the things he missed. You and the other sister, Babs, he thinks you're past helping, too set in your ways altogether, and the money'll just be a little luxury to you. But to Julie, that's a different matter. It will open all the doors to her that were closed to him. It will give her confidence as well as polish. That's what he wants. Split three ways the money can do a little bit for all of you, but kept in one lump sum it can do a lot for one! I'm sure you can see that.

Peggy It isn't fair. I've waited so long . . . (*Checking herself*) How do you know all this? He can't talk. You're just guessing.

Julian Partly it's guesswork, but he's confirmed it all. We play a little game. He manages to convey something to me, and I guess the rest. "Is it like this, Grandad?" I say, and he nods and winks. He can hear, even if he can't speak, and he's all right upstairs. No screws loose I can tell you.

Peggy He's in his right mind—you're sure about that?

Julian Absolutely sure.

Peggy (*with resignation*) Then that's that. He must do as he chooses. It's *his* money, after all.

Julian But it's so unfair. Think of what you could do with the money—
get married, put a nice fat deposit on a little house, and help your
fiancé with his business—now that would be something, wouldn't it?

Peggy (*ruefully*) It would have helped. We were expecting about fifteen
thousand each. I was counting on it to be honest. So was Howard,
though he wouldn't admit it.

Julian And after all you've done as well. (*He pours on the sympathy*)

Peggy (*reflectively, pacing across the room*) Yes, it's true. I've done more
than the others. The oldest always does. And now just because Julie is
going to Cambridge he leaves it all to her. I didn't have the opportunity of going on—not me—I had to leave school and go to work
whether I liked it or not. He wouldn't spare us a copper, the old skin-
flint—he said it was good for us to suffer . . . (*Almost forgetting Julian
in her agitation*) No, it isn't fair, it isn't fair! He said we had to make
our own way, the old man, just like he did, and he watched us go on
struggling, my mother and Babs and me. But now Julie, who's hardly
had to struggle at all, who's life has been made so much easier by *my*
efforts, she's to get all the money! And what am I to get? Nothing. I
might even lose Howard. Oh God, it isn't fair! (*She is almost in tears
and oblivious of Julian*)

Julian (*quietly*) There is a way round it.

Peggy (*coming back to reality with a start*) Oh—Mr Fudge. This must be
embarrassing you. I'm sorry I forgot myself for a moment . . .

Julian No, it's quite all right really. I'm used to—human emotions. I just
said that there is a way round this little problem.

Peggy A way round it—how?

Julian Supposing he left all his money to you, instead of to Julie?

Peggy That isn't possible. He's made up his mind. He never changes his
mind. You don't know him like I do.

Julian Oh, he won't change his mind, but I could change it for him.

Peggy What do you mean?

Julian He can't write now. He can just about scrawl his name, and that's
all he'll have to do. I'm to write the Will out for him. He's asked me to.
He trusts me, you see. Well, supposing I insert your name instead of
Julie's? He won't know. He can't see well enough to read small print.
He won't know what I've written.

Peggy (*shocked*) It isn't possible. It's—it's illegal.

Julian Like destroying the other Will—that was illegal, too, I believe!

Peggy You can't prove—you don't know I destroyed it. You're just guessing.

Julian You knew what was in it. Who else did?

Peggy I'm not admitting anything—anything. But what you suggest is
quite impossible. It's too dangerous. If anyone found out—Besides
you'd need another signature, have you thought of that? If you witness
it, you'll still need another signature.

Julian (*blandly*) Mrs Moore! Who could be better. She won't know what's
in it. She won't even ask.

Peggy (*tempted*) It wouldn't work—if we were caught.

Julian There's no way we could be caught. If the old man found out, somehow, which isn't likely, I could always say I misunderstood what he meant. After all, he can't speak! Who else understands him but me? It's foolproof.

Peggy It wouldn't be fair on the others—my sisters.

Julian You could give them a few thousand, just as a token of sisterly affection. You wouldn't even miss it.

Peggy And what about you? What would you get out of it? I'm sure you're not doing it for nothing.

Julian Not quite for nothing, no. I'd accept a small gift from you in recognition of my services—say five thousand pounds. Not much—considering.

Peggy Five thousand! That's a bit greedy!

Julian Oh, I don't think so. After all, you couldn't do it all without me. He trusts me. He doesn't trust you—not any more.

Peggy (*nervously*) I don't like it. It's dishonest!

Julian Isn't it a bit late to start worrying about honesty?

Peggy Besides, it would put me in your power for ever. You wouldn't be content with five thousand. You'd keep coming back for more, over and over again, until I didn't have any left.

Julian You'd just have to trust me.

Peggy I don't see how I can trust you. You've got this thing off pat. You've probably done it all before. Is it your stock-in-trade, ingratiating yourself with your dying patients, just to make sure a few little legacies come your way?

Julian I've been quite lucky in that respect, I must admit.

Peggy As I thought. (*Decisively*) No, Mr Fudge. I don't like your plan. I don't like it at all, and I certainly don't agree. My grandfather can do as he pleases with his money.

Julian Oh, that is a shame! A real shame. Because you won't have anything, you see, and when Howard finds out perhaps you won't even have him!

Peggy I resent that suggestion . . .

Banging is heard off

Julian Ah—my master's voice. He knows it's time for his football programme. Oh well, we'd finished our little conflab, hadn't we? Such a pity you couldn't see things my way—these fine principles! It must be such a disadvantage having such fine principles!

Julian goes out to the hall, calling

Coming, me old dear, don't worry. I'm coming!

Peggy, her face a mask of fury, paces up and down by the fireplace, she looks at herself in the mirror

Peggy (*groaning*) Oh, Howard—Howard . . .

Julian enters, pushing Mr Dalrymple in his wheel-chair. The old man is wearing pyjamas, and has a rug round his knees as before

Julian Here he is, all clean and tidy and ready for bed, just as soon as he's seen his football, bless him. I expect he'd like a little drink of milk, but you can manage that, can't you, Miss Strange? They look after you well, don't they, old man? Oh dear, she hasn't even turned the set on. Shall I do it?

Peggy Do stop fussing over him. I'll see to him.

Julian I'll see you on Monday, then. My day off tomorrow, Mr Dalrymple. I hope you don't miss me. We'll sort that little matter out on Monday, shall we? Then it will be off your mind.

Mr Dalrymple nods in answer

Peggy Don't be so sure you'll be here on Monday.

Julian Not thinking of giving me the sack, are you? I don't think you'll do that, Miss Strange, not if you think about it. You can't dismiss people for nothing, not nowadays, and I don't think you'd like me to tell Dr Marshall the reason, do you? That little conversation we had—that's better kept just between ourselves—don't you agree?

Peggy (*resentfully*) I suppose you're right.

Julian I thought you'd see it my way. So I'll be here on Monday as usual. 'Bye, then—have a nice week-end, won't you?

Julian goes off through the hall

Peggy (*darkly*) The same to you.

The front door slams. Mr Dalrymple motions towards the television set, and grunts

Oh, all right. (*She goes over to it, and switches it on, but before any noise comes through she turns to him and says reproachfully*) Oh, Grandad, why do you want to leave all your money to Julie? Why—can't you see it isn't fair!

Mr Dalrymple grunts and motions to her to move away from the television. The sound comes on. He watches it with obvious delight. Peggy stands looking at him, having moved away. She moves around restlessly like a caged animal, prowling and pacing, she is in great distress. She turns to look at him

Why couldn't you leave it as it is now? Why can't you? With all of us getting our fair share?

Mr Dalrymple ignores her completely

(*Still pacing*) It isn't fair. It isn't fair! (*She stops behind his chair. A thought occurs to her. She stares at the back of his head fixedly, then with a great effort of will comes up behind him and takes hold of the pillow behind his head*) Just making you comfortable, Grandad, that's all . . . (*She takes the pillow and swiftly puts it across his face, holding it down hard with both hands*)

Mr Dalrymple struggles feebly, as—

the CURTAIN *falls*

SCENE 2

The same. The following week, afternoon

Nothing is changed, except that the settee has been moved to the middle of the room, replacing the armchair, which is now against the wall beside the sideboard. Sherry and glasses are on the sideboard

As the CURTAIN *rises Julie is sitting gloomily on the settee, reading. Mrs Moore enters from the kitchen with a plate of sandwiches in one hand and a plate of cakes in the other. She puts them both down on the table*

Mrs Moore Not back, yet, then? I thought I 'eard them.

Julie I keep thinking I can hear a car as well, but it always drives past.

Mrs Moore Not very nice, is it, just waiting? (*She goes over to the window and looks out*) Such a rotten day, as well, all gloomy and overcast, like a storm was brewing. (*She shivers*) Not very nice. I keep thinking I should've laid a fire.

Julie No, it doesn't matter. We're depressed, that's why it seems so bleak in here. It isn't really.

Mrs Moore Perhaps not. Always depressing, aren't they, funerals?

Julie I feel so guilty now not going with them. But I just felt I couldn't stand it. I can still remember when Mother died . . .

Mrs Moore Don't think about it, duck. They understand—the others. It's an ordeal for a young girl like you to go to a funeral.

Julie Besides, I hadn't finished my packing. I'm going up this afternoon . . .

Mrs Moore Going *up*?

Julie To Cambridge.

Mrs Moore Oh yes, so you are. What a pity this had to happen just before you left.

Julie Yes, it has disrupted things. I mean, we knew he was old and he was going to die soon, but still it was a shock.

Mrs Moore It always is, when someone close to you dies. It's always a shock. 'Ard to believe, isn't it, that you'll never see them again? Not ever.

Julie It is hard to believe. (*She shivers*) It's funny, Mrs M., but I thought I heard a noise in there last night, in his room, a scratching noise . . .

Mrs Moore Perhaps you did.

Julie But no-one was in but me. I went and listened outside his door, and I'm sure I heard something, faintly—I couldn't make out what it was, but I hadn't the courage to go in and investigate. I'm a frightful coward.

Mrs Moore Could've been mice. They make a scratching noise.

Julie I hope not. I'm more afraid of mice than I am of ghosts.

There is the sound of a car drawing up outside. Mrs Moore goes over to the window and looks out

Mrs Moore It's them. They're 'ere. I'll go and put the kettle on.

Mrs Moore goes off to the kitchen

Julie looks towards the hall door. The front door slams

Babs, Peggy and Howard enter. They are all rather sombrely dressed, but not actually in black

Babs removes her hat and puts it on the table. Peggy goes to look at herself in the mirror, also removing her hat. Howard remains by the sideboard

Babs (*as she enters*) Thank God that's over!

Julie Was everything all right?

Babs Of course. As all right as a funeral can be. (*She sits next to Julie on the settee and forages in her handbag for a cigarette*)

Julie I should have come with you, really. I've felt just as bad staying here on my own—worse really.

Babs I'm glad you didn't come. It would have upset you, seeing him put down in that hole . . .

Peggy (*quickly*) Don't dwell on it. (*She too lights a cigarette*)

Babs (*surprised*) I wasn't going to.

Howard I'm surprised you didn't have him cremated. Seems much more hygienic to me.

Babs Oh, he didn't want to be burned. He gave us strict instructions about that. He said he'd have quite enough heat on the other side without preparing for it here.

Howard (*almost laughing*) That sounds like him!

Mrs Moore enters from the kitchen

Mrs Moore I'm just making the tea. Did everything go all right?

Peggy Yes, thanks, Mrs M.

Mrs Moore That's good.

Mrs Moore returns to the kitchen

Babs I don't know that I want tea, personally.

Peggy There's sherry on the sideboard.

Howard Yes, let's all have a sherry. I'll tell Mrs M. (*He goes to the kitchen door and calls off*) We've decided we'd rather have sherry, Mrs M.

Mrs Moore (*off*) Oh, all right—I'll just turn the kettle off.
Howard Shall I do the honours?
Peggy Please.

Howard begins to pour out sherry

Mrs Moore enters

Peggy Perhaps you'll join us, Mrs M.?
Mrs Moore Well, I wouldn't say no. It is a better idea, having sherry.
Warms you up, like. It's such a rotten day. You couldn't have had a
worse one for a funeral.
Babs It didn't actually rain.
Mrs Moore Oh, thank you. (*She takes the sherry from Howard and sits*)
Were there many there?

During the following, Howard pours out sherry and hands it round

Peggy No, just us. I think he'd outlived all his contemporaries.
Babs He'd had more than his three score years and ten.
Howard He'd enjoyed it all, too. He'd had a good life.
Peggy How do you know? I don't think any of us knew much about him
at all. I thought that during the service, how little we knew him. I sup-
pose how little we really know anyone.
Babs Ah, time for a philosophical break!
Peggy (*crossly*) Don't be so flippant, Babs.
Babs Just my nature, duckie! One thing I'm sure about, anyway, he would
not want us to mourn him. He said if we went into black he'd come
back and haunt us!
Mrs Moore (*laughing*) He would, too, he was that awkward. Not that I
want to speak ill of the dead!
Peggy I don't know why we're talking about him at all . . .
Howard He was a real character, you could say that for him!
Babs Character! He was impossible! I told him when I was a little girl
that he'd never go to heaven because he swore too much and he just
said that was good because he didn't know anyone there!

Howard, Babs and Mrs Moore laugh

Peggy (*explosively*) Will you stop talking about him!

They all turn and stare at her

Howard It's quite natural to talk about the dear departed just after the
funeral—surely.
Peggy I'm sorry. But you can see that Julie and I are upset.
Babs *You* certainly are, anyway.
Howard All right, let's just have one drink to him, and then talk about
something else. (*He solemnly raises his glass*) To the old man—wherever
he is!

*They all drink, with the exception of Peggy, who turns away and puts her
drink down on the mantelpiece*

Howard Now we'll change the subject. What shall we talk about?
Babs Perhaps we ought to play cards.
Howard Yes, he'd approve of that.
Babs Shush, we promised not to talk about him!
Howard Oh, sorry.

There is a pause

(*With an attempt at jocularity*) What are you all going to do with the money, that's what I want to know.
Peggy We haven't got it yet.
Howard But you will, won't you? It's only a formality, isn't it? Well, what are you going to do with it?
Babs I know what I'm going to do. A Greek holiday, that's my first and foremost little extravagance. Rounded off with a nice romance, I hope. Greek men are simply staggering, so I've heard. Anyway, we had a Greek doctor once at the hospital, who was quite delicious. He only spoke the most rudimentary English, but I must say it didn't cramp his style.
Peggy Really, Babs, must we suffer your lurid confessions?
Babs Who's confessin'? I'm boasting! Well, after I've had my holiday I shall buy a really super sports-car, streamlined and gorgeous to look at. After that—lots and lots of glamorous clothes . . .
Howard I should think your share will last you a few months at that rate! What about you, Julie? What plans have you got?
Julie None at all. I haven't thought about it. It will help me, of course, while I'm studying. Otherwise I just don't know.
Babs It will help you to get an even richer husband, my dear. Money attracts money, you know.
Howard I know Peggy's plans, so I won't ask.
Peggy Do you?
Howard The same as mine, aren't they?
Peggy You're very sure of yourself.
Howard (*puzzled*) Shouldn't I be?

They exchange glances. There is a pause

Mrs Moore I suppose you found the new Will all right then?
Peggy (*quickly*) New one . . . ?
Mrs Moore That's right. I told Mr Fudge to put it in his secret drawer, along with his other papers. Pity about Mr Fudge, isn't it? We won't see him any more, and I was quite getting to like him. Very friendly sort of person, wasn't he?
Peggy Yes, very. What did you mean about telling him where to put the Will?
Mrs Moore Last Saturday afternoon, Mr Fudge came round to my 'ouse and asked me if I'd come back 'ere and witness the old boy's signature, like I had before. So I did.
Peggy You didn't tell me.

Mrs Moore I thought he'd do that, Mr Fudge. He seemed to have taken charge of the old man.

Babs He didn't say anything, did he, Peggy?

Peggy Not to me.

Mrs Moore Perhaps he forgot! Anyway, you look in the drawer. It'll be there, I daresay!

Pause. Howard is about to say something, but Peggy shakes her head at him

Peggy We don't want to keep you, Mrs M. It was nice of you to pop round.

Mrs Moore Oh yes, all right, I'll be off. Charlie will be in pretty soon. (*She finishes her sherry and puts the glass down on the table*) Thank you for the drink, dears. It just filled a hole. (*She rises and goes over to the hall door*) I'll see meself out.

Mrs Moore goes out, shutting the door behind her

Babs What was she talking about—a new Will?

Peggy I don't know. I wish I did.

Howard Could there be another Will? What's the date on that one, the one you showed me this morning?

Peggy I'll fetch it.

Peggy goes off to the hall

Julie What does it mean?

Babs It could mean that the old b. hasn't left us a sou! What a joke if he decided to leave it to the poor and needy instead.

Howard I thought we were the poor and needy!

Babs I certainly am. I can't vouch for you.

Peggy enters with a Will in an envelope

Peggy Here it is. (*She takes it out of the envelope*) As you can see it's dated two years ago and witnessed by you, and that man who came round to do the gardening that year.

Howard (*taking it*) And there's no sign of another Will in there?

Peggy No.

Howard I wonder what the old bird was getting at.

Babs Perhaps she had a mental aberration.

Peggy I don't know, I'm sure. It's all very depressing and disturbing. This week has been hell . . . (*She sits disconsolately*)

Julie Yes it has. (*She rises suddenly*) And frankly I shall be glad to get away. I don't care if there's any money or not. I intend to make my own way in the world whatever happens. I hate all this speculation about money. It's so sordid. (*She goes up to the hall door. They all look at her with some surprise*) I'm going to finish my packing now. Perhaps,

Howard, you wouldn't mind giving me a lift to the station? There's a
train in about half-an-hour.

Howard I'd be glad to—you know that.

Julie All right then. I won't be long.

Julie goes out to the hall

Babs What brought that on?

Peggy I don't know. I suppose she's more upset about all this than we
realized.

Babs Funny, she seemed so grown-up all of a sudden talking like that.
She's going places all right. She's got drive and that's really more important than brains.

Howard She's good looking, too.

Babs Oh, you've noticed! There's life in the old dog yet, Peggy, you'd
better watch him!

Peggy (*crossly*) Oh do stop it—all this levity! I don't know how you can,
today of all days!

Babs I'd rather laugh than cry. Besides, I feel a bit light-headed with that
bombshell Mrs Moore has just released! Supposing there is another
Will? Perhaps we ought to look for it.

Peggy (*desperately*) Must we? Isn't it better to leave things the way they
are?

Howard Better—but is it strictly honest?

Peggy It would be terrible to lose it just when it's within our grasp—all
that money!

Babs I thought it was too much to hope for! Bang goes my Greek holiday!

Howard There's no reason to suppose that the second Will is any different
from the first.

Peggy It must be, or he wouldn't have made it.

Howard I hadn't thought of that. (*Sitting by the table*) Does anyone want
a sandwich? I'm starving. (*He takes a sandwich*)

Peggy How can you think of eating at a time like this? You're thoroughly
insensitive.

Howard I'm not insensitive. I'm just hungry! Anyway, I agree with Babs,
the old boy wouldn't appreciate us mourning. He'd think it was plain
stupid. And as far as the Will is concerned and old Mother Moore, she
probably just made a mistake. She might have been signing for something else, for Mr Fudge to go and draw the old boy's pension or something like that. You know how muddled she gets things.

Peggy Not that muddled. Even she knows the difference between a will
form and a pension book.

Babs Personally I can't help thinking it's the old boy's sense of humour.
He's laughing at us somewhere, I shouldn't be surprised!

Howard (*laughing*) You're right there . . .

Peggy (*explosively*) Oh, do stop it. How can you talk like that!

They both look at her in stunned silence

Babs I didn't mean it . . .

Howard She was joking, Peg.

Peggy (*rushing over to the hall door*) I've had enough jokes for one day—my head aches . . .

Peggy rushes out, slamming the door behind her

Howard (*after a pause*) Poor old Peg, she does seem overwrought today.

Babs Her nerves are in a shocking state at the moment, Howard. She was bad enough before, but since the old boy pegged it she's been darn sight worse. She cries a lot, you can see that by her eyes, and this morning she said to me she had a horrible dream when she heard the old man banging on the floor for attention like he used to. She was very upset by it. I could tell.

Howard Poor girl! She's had a rough time lately. I haven't helped matters, though.

Babs No, you haven't. Have you sorted out your problems yet, over that other woman—the blonde?

Howard (*surprised*) You know about it, too?

Babs It's difficult to keep secrets in this house.

Howard (*hesitantly*) Well, it wasn't really a problem at all. Peggy made too much of it.

Babs (*pointedly*) Did she?

Howard (*evasively*) You know how it is, Babs . . .

Babs A man's a man for a' that, you mean?

Howard Yes, I suppose I do.

Babs It upset Peggy though.

Howard Yes, it was a bit thoughtless of me. We had a terrible row last week, the very day he died, actually. But as soon as I'd heard what had happened I came round like a shot. You see, Babs, it's been two years now and I really do care about your sister, whether she believes it or not.

Babs Yes, I'm sure you do. You'll be all right once you get married. You've waited too long.

Howard It wasn't *my* idea!

Babs And now you'll have a nice little sum to start you off. Money and love—it can't be bad! (*She stretches*) God, but I'm tired! I'm on duty tonight as well.

Howard Oh, bad luck! Couldn't you have got a night off?

Babs I didn't want to use up my precious off-duty going to a funeral, mate, I can assure you. No, I'll manage. I must go to bed soon, though, and have a few hours' kip before tonight.

There is a knock at the front door

Babs Who can that be? I'm not in the mood for visitors.

Peggy (*off*) It's all right, I'll go.

Voices are heard in the hall, then the door opens

It's Mr Fudge.

*Peggy and Julian enter. Peggy comes into the room, leaving Julian stand-
ing by the sideboard. Howard rises and goes up to him*

Julian I was just saying that I went to the cemetery but you'd already left.
I must have mistaken the time. I put some flowers on the grave.
Babs How nice of you!
Julian I always do that when my old people go, just a gesture!
Babs It must get expensive!
Julian (*sharply*) Not all my patients die, Miss Strange. I wouldn't want
you to think that.
Babs I didn't mean to imply it.

A slight pause

Howard Would you like a drink, Mr Fudge? I'm afraid it's only sherry.
Julian Oh, thank you, that suits me fine. I only drink sherry.
Howard That's all right then. (*He pours Julian a drink and takes it over*)
Julian I do hope I'm not intruding, but I wanted to pop in and pay my
condolences. It came rather suddenly, didn't it, the end? I'm sorry I
wasn't here to help you.
Babs We managed.
Julian It must have been just after I left. Funny that, because I'd taken
his pulse and given him his medicine. I would have thought he was
as right as ninepence until Monday morning. It just shows you, you
never can tell about these things. I was quite staggered when Dr Marshall rang and told me the old boy had gone. But, of course, at his age
and with him being ill for so long one had to expect it. There would
be no need for an inquest. Dr Marshall made that quite clear.
Peggy (*sharply*) Inquest? Why should there be an inquest?
Julian That's what I'm saying. There was no need. Still, he didn't have
another stroke, did he, the old boy? He just simply gave up and went to
sleep. At least that's the way I heard it. He didn't seem to me to be
the giving-up sort. But we can all be wrong.
Peggy You didn't know him very well, Mr Fudge. You were only here a
week.
Julian (*significantly*) Yes, but I'm very intuitive, you see, Miss Strange.
I get to know people *very* quickly.

Peggy is disconcerted by this remark, and turns away

Julie appears in the hall doorway with two suitcases

Julie I'm ready.
Howard Righto—so am I! (*He moves to the hall door*)
Babs (*going up to Julie*) You don't mind if I don't come to the station with
you, do you, duckie? I must get off to bed. I'm on duty tonight.
Julie No, I don't mind at all. I'd rather say good-bye here. I hate station
platform good-byes.

Peggy So do I.

Peggy goes up to the doorway as Babs, Julie and Howard disappear into the passage

Excuse us a minute, Mr Fudge.

Babs, Julie, Howard and Peggy go off to the hall

Julian Of course.
Babs (*off*) Lots of luck. You'll knock 'em dead up there, Julie. Don't worry about a thing.
Peggy (*off*) Lots of luck, darling. I know you'll make good.
Julie (*off*) Good-bye, then.
Peggy⎫
Babs ⎬ (*off*) Good-bye . . . ⎱ (*Speaking together*)

The front door slams. A car starts up and drives away

Babs enters

Babs I shall miss her. I feel quite choked . . . (*She blows her nose hard and then looks pointedly at Julian*) I'm sorry, we're not very hospitable, Mr Fudge. You caught us at a bad time. (*She yawns*)
Julian Sorry, I'm sure!

Peggy enters

Peggy It's all right, Babs. I want to have a word with Mr Fudge anyway. You go up to bed.
Babs Thanks, I will. (*She goes and picks up her handbag and hat*) I don't suppose I'll see you again, Mr Fudge—so good-bye.
Julian Good-bye, then. It's been nice knowing you.

Babs grimaces at him behind his back and then goes off to the hall

Julian You wanted to have a word with me. Well, how nice!
Peggy (*uneasily*) I wondered if you could clear up a little mystery for me, since you're so fond of mysteries.
Julian I'll try.
Peggy Mrs Moore said something we couldn't quite understand, about signing a new Will on Saturday afternoon, *last* Saturday.
Julian That's right. I have it here. (*He pats his pocket*)
Peggy Have you forgotten our conversation that day? What you said to me.
Julian Not at all. I told a little white lie, you see. I pretended the old boy was going to make out a new Will on Monday when in fact he'd already done it. I thought it put me in a better bargaining position telling you that, made you feel that it was in my power to alter it, so to speak.
Peggy (*frostily*) Do you mind letting me see it?

Julian Not at all. That's why I came, really. (*He hands it to her*) As you will see, you're a very lucky girl.

Peggy stands by the fireplace, reading the Will

I hope you'll forgive my little subterfuge. It was just a game. I meant no harm by it, none at all. I had no idea the effect it would have on you, you see . . .

Peggy (*scarcely aware of him*) He's left it to me! To me! (*She sits down with the shock*) I can't believe it. Are you sure this is legal? It isn't a forgery?

Julian Of course it isn't a forgery. It's perfectly legal. Take it to a solicitor and have it proved if you like. It's all perfectly legal. That's his own fair hand—not mine.

Peggy Why did you tell me all that last week? Why did you want me to believe he was going to leave it to Julie?

Julian I've already explained that, my dear. We all have the right to feather our own nest, given the opportunity.

Peggy But I don't understand. Julie was his favourite. He never cared much for me.

Julian Perhaps you didn't know him as well as you thought. He was very proud of Julie, that's true, but after he'd been in hospital he thought it all out again, and I think he decided that you were the one who'd use the money more sensibly than the others. (*He pauses, looking at her shrewdly*) I think he knew you'd destroyed the other Will—now, don't deny it—but it didn't dismay him, not at all. He admired courage and strength. He realized that you had to do something like that—daring and unprincipled. I think it amused him!

Peggy (*distraught*) Oh God, it isn't what I want—it really isn't what I want. It isn't right. It isn't *just*.

Julian What's the matter? Remorse setting in?

Peggy (*recovering herself*) What do you mean, remorse?

Julian You're not going to pretend to me that the old boy died a natural death, are you?

Peggy Of course he did, what are you suggesting?

Julian What did you do? Give him an extra dose of morphia?

Peggy I don't know what you mean. I don't know anything about drugs.

Julian He's got enough pills in there to see off an elephant, but no, I suppose you wouldn't know what to give him, not without asking your sister and you'd hardly do that. So what did you do, then? A cord round the neck, no, the marks would show. Something soft and easy . . . (*He looks round the room*)

Peggy (*rising, hysterically*) You don't know what you're saying . . . How dare you suggest such a thing?

Julian Something soft and easy. (*He looks at the settee*) Yes, a cushion or a pillow—that would do, wouldn't it? That would finish him. He was a weak old man, he wouldn't take long to suffocate. How did you feel when you were pushing down on his face, knowing you were choking the life out of him, your own grandfather. How did it feel?

Peggy Stop tormenting me like this!

Julian Yes, all right, I will. I'm sure I don't want to torment anybody. *I'm* not cruel. Just give me my money, and I won't bother you a moment longer.

Peggy What money?

Julian The money you promised me on Saturday.

Peggy I promised you nothing.

Julian Now don't be awkward. (*He sits down as if he intends to stay*) I made a little proposition to you, and I gather you accepted it.

Peggy If you mean changing the Will you know very well I didn't accept it. You were trying to make me party to a criminal act, a forgery—when all the time you knew the contents of the Will. You knew he'd left the money to me, anyway. I don't owe you a thing, Mr Fudge, and the sooner you go the better!

Julian (*amiably*) Oh, you are being unpleasant to me, Miss Strange, and I'm sure I don't deserve it. You can't blame a man for trying to feather his nest when he sees the opportunity. I realize I came unstuck there, but then I just didn't realize how desperate you were. (*Pause*) Now, however, I'm in an even better bargaining position. (*Slowly*) You see, I know that you killed the old boy.

Peggy You don't know anything. You're guessing. You haven't any proof!

Julian Proof? Only guilty people talk about proof. Anyway, I could easily find some proof. You should have had him cremated. I only have to whisper a few words in the right ear to have him exhumed. You'd be surprised what a body can reveal after it's dead.

Peggy You mean a post-mortem?

Julian That's right.

Peggy They wouldn't find anything. How could they?

Julian Quite easily, my dear. The lungs being in a collapsed state—that would immediately suggest suffocation. There might be tiny pieces of feather or thread inhaled from the article—whatever it was you used. He could easily have drawn something like that into his lungs while he was gasping for breath. His finger-nails, too. What might they not find under his finger-nails beneath a microscope? I expect he struggled for his life.

Peggy Stop—stop . . . (*She puts her hands over her ears*) I don't want to hear any more. Stop it, stop it . . .

Julian I will stop. I've told you that. Just give me my money, that's all you have to do. Five thousand pounds, I think, was the agreed sum. Cheap at the price.

Peggy You're bluffing. You don't really know anything at all.

Julian (*rising*) All right, then—call my bluff!

There is a pause. They stand looking at each other—antagonists

Peggy You know you can go to prison for blackmail.

Julian So you can for murder, my dear, ten years at least!

Peggy Ten years!

Julian Yes, imagine that! You wouldn't be very young when you came out, would you? Howard wouldn't wait for you, not he! And there wouldn't be any money either, because a murderer cannot benefit from her victim's estate. (*Pause*) So I really don't think you have much choice, do you?

Peggy Why are you doing this to me? Why do you want to hurt me?

Julian (*with sudden viciousness*) I'm the Avenging Angel, that's why. I liked that old man, believe it or not, and I don't like to think of him struggling to breathe while his own granddaughter suffocated him to death! How do you think he felt, poor old soul, all the time he was dying, knowing that you were killing him?

Peggy Oh God, what am I to do? (*She wanders about, distraught*) Last night I couldn't sleep. I thought I heard him, banging on the floor with his stick just like he used to. I did hear him. I did.

Julian Perhaps you did. They say the murdered don't sleep soundly!

There is a knock at the front door. Peggy starts, and almost screams. She stares frantically at the hall door

(*Soothingly*) I expect it's Howard, back from the station.

Peggy (*relieved*) Of course, of course, Howard . . . You'd better go. He'd throw you out if he knew . . .

Julian He'd throw you out, wouldn't he? If he knew!

Peggy glares at Julian, then goes off to the hall

There is another knock on the door. Julian picks up the Will from the table and puts it in his pocket

Howard (*off*) I wondered where you were.

Howard and Peggy enter

Peggy We were just discussing some business, Mr Fudge and I. I'm sorry to keep you waiting.

Howard Oh, is Mr Fudge still here?

Julian I'm just going. I'll call again tomorrow, Miss Strange, about the cheque.

Peggy Yes, all right.

Julian Don't bother to see me out, I know the way. I must admit I have enjoyed working in this household. It's been *very* rewarding.

Peggy That's good.

Julian I daresay I can quote your name as a reference.

Peggy (*shortly*) Of course.

Julian Good-bye then, until tomorrow. I'll call early, around ten o'clock. I have so much to do. I'm thinking of going away, you see, on a long trip. I feel as if I need a rest. Cheeribye . . .

Julian goes off to the hall

Peggy Good-bye.

The front door slams. Peggy breathes a sigh of relief

Howard (*curiously*) Is anything wrong, Peggy? What was all the business about a cheque?

Peggy Oh, just some money we owe him from last week.

Howard I see. Could he explain what Mrs Moore meant about signing another Will? You did ask him, I suppose?

Peggy Yes, yes, I asked him. It was just as you said. Nothing to do with a Will at all. It was some other paper that needed a witness—something to do with extra benefit. Yes, that was it. The old man was entitled to extra benefit because of having a constant attendant here, you see.

Howard Oh good! So there's nothing to worry about after all.

Peggy No, no, not a thing.

Howard Is there anything else wrong? You seem a bit nervous, on edge about something.

Peggy No, there's nothing else wrong. It's just that today has been such a strain . . .

Howard Of course it has. You sit down and put your feet up and I'll make you a nice cup of tea.

Peggy Thank you, I will. (*She sits down on the settee and Howard fusses around her, making her comfortable*)

Howard I suppose we can start looking for a house tomorrow.

Peggy Yes, we can at last!

Howard is about to go off into the kitchen when she calls him back

Howard . . .

Howard Yes?

Peggy (*hesitantly*) Would you still care for me if I'd done something awful? Something you didn't approve of.

Howard I can't imagine you doing anything I didn't approve of—not with your high principles!

Peggy But if I did!

Howard (*coming back to her*) It wouldn't worry me a scrap. I don't want a perfect woman. I want another fallible human being, like myself. (*He kisses her gently*) Now, I'll make the tea . . .

Peggy (*clinging to him*) I shall be all alone in this house tonight. I don't think I can face it.

Howard No, Babs said you'd been having nightmares.

Peggy More—much worse than nightmares! So real! (*She shudders*) Oh, Howard, stay with me tonight.

Howard (*surprised*) What will the neighbours say?

Peggy To hell with the neighbours. I need you—near me . . .

Howard All right then. That suits me. As long as you're sure . . .

Peggy I am—quite sure.

They kiss as—

the CURTAIN *falls*

ACT III

The same. The following morning

As the CURTAIN *rises, Babs enters from the kitchen in her nurse's uniform, carrying a cup of tea. She sits at the table, takes a cigarette from her bag which is on the table, and lights it. Howard enters from the hall in his shirt-sleeves, looking dishevelled. He carries a morning paper and his coat*

Babs (*surprised*) Oh, hallo!

Howard Good morning. I thought I heard someone down here. Made some tea, have you? (*He puts his coat on the back of the settee*)

Babs Yes, in the kitchen.

Howard goes through into the kitchen and returns after a minute with a cup of tea

What a surprise to see you here at this time of day.

Howard (*sitting at the table*) I stayed here last night.

Babs I gathered that.

Howard Peggy didn't want to be alone.

Babs My God, she had to make up an excuse!

Howard No, it wasn't like that. I suppose she feels, now that Julie's gone, to hell with appearances. She even said that—to hell with the neighbours.

Babs Wonders will never cease! And are you going to be a permanent lodger here now?

Howard Oh, I don't think so.

Babs Not that I mind. I'd just like to know.

Howard No, really, I don't think so. It won't be long now before we can set up our own home, I suppose.

Babs You don't sound very enthusiastic.

Howard To be honest, Babs, I feel like a little boy who's waited and waited for a clockwork train for Christmas, and when it finally comes—well, it's a bit of a let-down, really.

Babs What a fine way to describe your forthcoming marriage!

Howard It's not that exactly. I don't *mean* that. I mean the way we've waited for the money all this time. We've made it too important. I wish to God we'd married when we first met—that was the best time. Now—frankly, Babs, the gloss has gone off it. It'll be a bit like marrying my own sister. We know each other too well.

Babs You really should tell Peggy this, not me.

Howard I know. I shall try.

Babs I've made up my mind what I'm going to do anyway. I handed in my notice last night.

Howard Good God, that was a bit rash, wasn't it? You haven't got the money yet.

Babs I can't help that. I had a row with the Night Sister and told her what to do with the job. Just think of it—one more month, and I'm free!

Howard (*enviously*) There'll be no holding you then.

Babs I should think not. I'll go on a cruise, I think, and spend money like water. Who knows, I might meet a fascinating millionaire and be set up for life, just like an old movie!

Howard I didn't know you had such imagination!

Babs Oh, we all have our Castles in the Air!

Howard That's all right, as long as they remain there—in the air. When they come down to earth they look a bit different.

Babs You are in an odd mood, Howard. Not a bit like your old self. I do believe you're getting cold feet about losing your bachelorhood. I never would have thought it!

Howard (*darkly*) Neither would I.

Babs (*rising*) I think I need another cup of tea to fortify me—do you?

Howard Not yet, thanks.

Babs (*moving to the kitchen*) Cheer up, Chicken. It may never happen!

Babs exits to the kitchen

Howard tries to read his paper, but after a moment is staring moodily over the top of it

Peggy enters from the hall. She is smartly dressed

Peggy Is Babs in? I thought I heard voices.

Howard Yes, she's in the kitchen. (*He rises and tries to kiss her*)

Peggy (*backing away from him*) Don't you think you should have a shave? You look rather a mess.

Howard I usually have a cup of tea and surface a bit first.

Peggy I'd much rather you surfaced afterwards.

Howard (*disgruntled*) All right. (*He puts down his paper*)

Howard exits to the hall

Peggy begins to tidy up the room

Babs enters with two cups of tea

Babs I heard you, so I've brought you a cuppa.

Peggy Thanks very much.

They both sit down at the table

Babs Where's Howard?

Peggy I sent him off to shave.

Babs Oh—did he tell you?

Peggy Tell me what?

Babs That I'd given in my notice. I shall leave at the end of the month.

Peggy No, he didn't tell me. That's a bit reckless, isn't it?

Babs Well, there shouldn't be any difficulty over the Will, should there?
If there is I can always borrow some money. I'm an heiress now. We
all are. It does give one a nice, comfortable feeling, I must say. I wonder
how much there is?

Peggy Fifty thousand pounds, divided three ways. You work it out!

Babs I suppose there's tax to pay on that. Still—about what? fifteen or
sixteen thousand. Very nice!

Peggy Yes.

Babs You don't sound a bit thrilled! What has got in to everyone today?

Peggy What do you mean—everyone?

Babs I thought Howard was a bit down in the mouth, too.

Peggy Oh? I hadn't noticed.

Babs What's your trouble, then?

Peggy (*sighing*) My usual trouble—dreams.

Babs Even with Howard here?

Peggy Even with Howard here—I still heard something in the night.
I was sure I heard it again—the knocking. (*She shivers*) I did, I did
hear it. I wasn't dreaming.

Babs (*gently*) Of course you were.

Peggy (*desperately*) No, it wasn't a dream, I was wide awake and I heard
him knocking.

Babs Really, Peg, I'm beginning to think you ought to see a psychiatrist.

Peggy I did hear it, I did! I even came down here and listened at the door.
(*She shudders*) I was so frightened I was quivering all over, but I still
had to force myself to come downstairs and listen.

Babs Did Howard hear anything?

Peggy I haven't asked him.

Babs Let's be sensible, Peg. It's all in your mind. It must be. Of course
it seems very real to you. I'm not suggesting you're making it up, but
the fact remains that it is quite impossible, and you know it really.

Peggy I suppose you're right.

Babs Of course, I am.

Peggy Will you do one thing for me, though? Will you go in there and
clear away his things—that old stick of his, things like that?

Babs When?

Peggy This morning—now.

Babs But I'm tired—I've been on duty all night!

Peggy Please, Babs . . .

Babs Oh, all right. I'll see what I can do for you. (*She rises and goes
over to the hall door*) I'll have a quick tidy up, but I'm not turning out
every drawer and cupboard. I'm too tired for that.

Peggy Yes, all right, thank you. It's that stick mainly . . .

Howard comes in just as Babs is going out. She strokes his chin

Babs Oh, lovely! Just like a baby's bottom!

Babs goes out to the hall

Howard Where's she going? To bed without anything to eat?

Peggy No, she's going to clear out some of Grandad's things in there.

Howard Oh, that's a job that had to be faced some time, I suppose. (*He sits down at the table*)

Peggy Do you want another cup of tea?

Howard Not just yet, thank you. There's something I'd like to talk about.

Peggy Yes?

Howard It's difficult. I don't quite know where to start.

Peggy (*apprehensively*) What's wrong?

Howard (*hesitantly*) Well, now that you have got the money and everything, there's nothing to stop us getting married . . .

Peggy No, there isn't . . .

Howard But I don't think we should be in too much of a hurry, that's all . . .

Peggy After two years we can hardly be accused of being impetuous!

Howard No, I know that—but the trouble is, I wonder if we haven't waited too long already . . .

Peggy What do you mean?

Howard It isn't the same, is it? It just isn't the same as it used to be in the beginning. There isn't any fire.

Peggy You're talking like an adolescent, Howard. I thought you were more mature. Surely our relationship doesn't require—fire.

Howard Oh, but it does, Peggy. At any rate for me.

Peggy What are you getting at?

Howard Just that we ought to think about it before we commit ourselves finally, that's all.

Peggy What's brought this on all of a sudden. (*Suspiciously*) It's that other woman, isn't it? It's *her*.

Howard (*evasively*) Not exactly.

Peggy You don't sound very sure.

Howard To be honest it has made me see things differently meeting her. She's so warm, and quite frankly, you're not . . .

Peggy But I love you . . .

Howard Hollow words, I'm afraid. You neither love nor want me. I've suspected for some time that all you really want is a husband to give you security and respectability, but you don't want a man. At any rate, not me!

Peggy (*desperately*) That's silly. I have security now. I'm quite well off. Think of the money, Howard. Think of the plans we've made. Think of what we can do with the money.

Howard Don't degrade yourself. Peggy. It isn't like you.

Peggy Degrade myself? Oh, if you only knew what I've done! (*She is crushed, and huddles up in despair*)

Howard I'm sorry. (*He puts on his coat from the back of the settee*) I'd better go. We can't go on talking about it. It's getting us nowhere.

Peggy But you'll come back. It isn't over—please, Howard, don't say it's over. I just don't know what I'll do without you.

Howard I didn't say it was over. I said we should think about it.

Peggy I'll be so good to you, darling. (*She goes over to him, fawning on him*) You can have anything you like. I'll spend all the money on you, if you like—only don't leave me, particularly now—don't leave me . . .

Howard (*getting exasperated*) I've got to go to work . . .

Peggy I don't mean now. I mean don't leave me for ever. I just couldn't bear it, darling. You'll come back. Say you'll come back—I need you so.

Howard I'll see. I don't know. You're making this very hard for me, Peg.

Peggy I won't give you up, I just won't. I'm sorry I was jealous. You can have her if you like, the other woman. You can have her after we're married—only please don't leave me for good. I couldn't bear it.

Howard Will you shut up about the other woman!

Peggy But that's what it's about, isn't it? You were all right until you met her. It's all because of *her*.

Howard It isn't because of her at all. It's because of you. (*He moves to the hall door*)

Peggy (*following him*) Think of the money, Howard, think of the money.

Howard (*finally exasperated*) No amount of money could make up to me for sleeping with a corpse!

Peggy A corpse! (*She recoils from him in horror*)

Howard I'm sorry, Peg. I didn't mean it . . .

Peggy (*hurt and turning away from him*) Go away—go away . . .

Howard I'm sorry.

He waits for a moment, hoping she will turn round, but she does not

Oh, hell!

Howard goes, slamming the door. The front door slams

Peggy collapses on to the settee, moaning, hurt and bewildered

After a moment Babs appears in the hall doorway, pushing a wheel-chair with some old clothes in the seat, and a rug. On top of this pile is a cardboard box containing a selection of medicines

Babs I've done the best I can. There's plenty of rubbish left, but this will do to be going on with.

Peggy (*turning round, startled*) Where did you get that chair?

Babs Don't you remember, Mr Fudge got it for the old man? It was lent by the Red Cross. I thought perhaps you could take it back. Also all these clothes. Some of them are in quite good condition. They might be able to use them.

Peggy Yes, yes, all right.

Babs leaves the wheel-chair just above the table, then takes the cardboard box and puts it on the table

Babs These are all his old drugs. They ought to be thrown away.
Peggy All right—later.
Babs (*looking at her curiously*) Is anything wrong? Where's Howard?
Peggy He's gone.
Babs Gone?
Peggy (*with an effort*) Of course. He had to go to work.
Babs Oh yes, I didn't realize the time. (*She looks at her watch*) I'm later than usual. You're not going in, I take it?
Peggy No, I told them I wanted the rest of the week off. I can't face work at the moment. I sleep so badly . . .
Babs Yes, I know. The rest will do you good. (*She goes over to the kitchen*) I'll go and make myself some toast and a hot drink and then off to bed if you don't mind.
Peggy Of course I don't mind.
Babs (*hesitating in the doorway*) Funny old Howard not even saying good-bye.
Peggy He—er shouted out, but I suppose you didn't hear him.
Babs Did he? I must be going deaf!

Babs goes into the kitchen

Peggy goes over to the table where Babs has left the cardboard box and begins to examine the contents. She picks up a couple of bottles and goes over to the kitchen door

Peggy Babs . . .
Babs (*off*) Yes?
Peggy I was thinking perhaps we had better keep some of these. After all we often need sleeping-pills ourselves.

Babs comes to the doorway

Babs No, really, it's not a good idea to keep old drugs. If you want anything you should go to the doctor yourself.
Peggy (*holding up a bottle*) Are these very strong?
Babs (*coming over and looking at it*) This one is Nembutal, and the other one's Mogadon—yes, they're both quite strong. I think Dr Marshall was over-prescribing. The old man moaned so much—I expect that's why. I doubt whether he took them though. You know what he was like—plain awkward!
Peggy Yes—so you think we ought to throw them away?
Babs Throw them away or take them back to the chemist—wait a tick, I'll turn my toast over.

Babs goes off to the kitchen

Peggy goes back to the table, thoughtfully replaces the bottles, then she picks up another one, a large medicine bottle containing a brownish-yellow liquid

Peggy What's this stuff—in the bottle?

Babs comes to the doorway

Babs Oh, that's Nembutal elixir. I remember the doctor prescribing that. The old boy moaned that he couldn't manage the pills any more, said they stuck in his throat. That's deadly stuff. Real knock-out drops— that should be the first thing you chuck away!

Babs goes back into the kitchen

Peggy takes the top off the bottle and sniffs it. Then she puts the cap back and puts the bottle back in the box. She takes the box and puts it on the sideboard. Then she collects the cups that are on the table

Peggy exits to the kitchen

Peggy (*off*) I thought I'd better clear up a bit. I'm expecting someone this morning.
Babs (*off*) Oh, who?

Peggy and Babs come in together. Babs is eating a slice of toast and carrying a glass of milk

Peggy The insurance man—about Grandad's insurance.
Babs More money—that's good!
Peggy It won't be much! We have to pay for the funeral and everything.
Babs Every little counts! Well, if you're expecting somebody I'll retire right now. I'm so tired. I'll sleep like the dead today, that's for sure! (*She goes over to the hall door, munching her toast, then she turns and looks at Peggy anxiously*) You will be all right, won't you?
Peggy Of course. I'm quite all right in the day-time. It's the nights I can't stand.
Babs Sorry, duckie, there's not much I can do about that. Never mind, Howard will be here to keep you company tonight, won't he?
Peggy (*stiffly*) Oh yes—Howard will be here. Naturally Howard will be here.
Babs Good night, then, or rather good morning. See you around five.
Peggy O.K. Have a good rest.
Babs I intend to—dreaming of a blissful future! No work for at least six months—whoopee!

Babs goes off to the hall

Peggy looks after her thoughtfully, goes over to the door and opens it cautiously, looking off to make sure Babs has gone. Then she comes back into the room, sighs: "Oh, Howard, how could you, how could you?" She looks bleak momentarily, then she shrugs off this mood and with purpose goes over to the sideboard and takes the sherry from the top of it. She brings it back to the table. The decanter is about a quarter full. She tips the contents of the Nembutal elixir into the decanter, mixing it up. She puts it back on the sideboard, and puts the other drugs away in the sideboard cupboard. Having done this, she sits down on the settee, facing front, her face takes on a tense but dreamy expression as if she is day-dreaming. There is a loud knock at the front door, which startles her. She gets up, goes over to the window and looks out

Peggy exits to the hall; there is a murmur of voices, then she returns with Julian

Peggy (*as they enter*) You don't mind being quiet, do you? Babs has just gone to bed, and she's so tired.

Julian I've no intention of being noisy, my dear. Our little business won't take long, will it?

Peggy No, of course not. Won't you sit down?

Julian (*sitting on the settee*) Thought it over, have you? My little proposition.

Peggy Yes, I've thought it over. I can see it all in a different light this morning.

Julian I thought perhaps you would.

Peggy You were right really. Why shouldn't I have all the money? He wanted me to. Besides he owed it to me. They all owe me something—for the life I've given them.

Julian Exactly—I understand.

Peggy Do you? I've given all my life to the family. I didn't have the opportunity that Julie's had, otherwise—who knows . . .? (*She sighs bitterly*)

Julian That's the awful thing about self-sacrifice, isn't it? You just can't help resenting it. It really makes you much happier to be selfish, like I am, but you see you have to be strong to be selfish.

Peggy Strong? Don't you think I am strong?

Julian Because of what you did to the old man? Oh, that was the strength born of desperation, though, and instantly regretted, I daresay? (*Pause*) You won't *admit* anything. I don't blame you for that.

Peggy There's nothing to admit.

Julian Then why pay me off? Why not let me take my little suspicions to the police?

Peggy I just want to avoid a scandal, that's all.

Julian Oh, I see. Well, you're prepared to pay quite handsomely just to avoid a scandal, I must say. Five thousand pounds.

Peggy Yes—all right.

Julian (*pleased*) Here you are then. (*He rises and takes the Will over to* *her*) Make it known. Your sisters won't like it at first, but I don't suppose you'll be too miserly with them. Spare them the odd crust . . .

Peggy I fully intend to look after them. (*She takes the Will from him*) What do I do with it? Howard was the executor of the other one.

Julian It's quite simple. Just take it along to a solicitor with the old boy's death certificate and something to prove your identity, he'll do the rest.

Peggy And now you want your cheque?

Julian That's the general idea.

Peggy You do realize that I haven't any money to cover it at the moment?

Julian I'll wait. It won't take long. You can make it out just the same.

Peggy All right. (*She picks up her handbag from nearby the fireplace, and takes out her cheque book. Then she hesitates*) Perhaps we could have a little drink? I feel as if I need one.

Julian It is a bit early.

Peggy Just one—to seal the deal, as it were.

Julian Oh, all right. I don't mind a sherry.

Peggy That's all we've got. (*She goes over to the sideboard and begins to pour out two drinks from the decanter, with her back to him*) You said something about going away?

Julian (*sitting at the table*) That's right. A little cruise. I haven't a job at the moment, and your contribution will just set me up for the winter. I'll have to wait for it to come through, of course, but that shouldn't take long.

Peggy (*returning with glasses, concealing her own which has only a minute quantity*) Here's to your holiday. (*She hands him his drink, and sits down opposite to him, watching him. He does not drink at once*) Have you any family, Mr Fudge?

Julian Nobody to speak of. I'm all on my lonesome. I have *friends*, of course.

Peggy Yes, I thought you might have. But you live alone?

Julian Yes, I live alone. I have a nice little flat opposite the Market. I bother nobody and nobody bothers me. (*Leaning forward*) I must say you're suddenly very solicitous. I wonder why!

Peggy (*flustered*) I was only—making conversation.

Julian Don't bother. Let me just have the cheque.

Peggy Yes, of course. (*She hunts in her handbag for a pen*) You don't seem to like the sherry.

Julian I haven't tasted it yet. (*He does so, and pulls a face*)

Peggy Now, who should I make this out to? Julian Fudge, is that sufficient? (*She begins to write the cheque*)

Julian That's right. (*He takes another sip of the sherry, and then sniffs it*)

Peggy (*looking up*) You don't like it?

Julian Is it the same one you had out yesterday?

Peggy nods

Funny thing, it tastes quite different, and the smell—well, there's something familiar about the smell but I don't connect it with sherry. I'm no expert on drinks, mind you. Have you had it long?

Peggy No, we bought it for the funeral.

Julian Then I'd take it back if I were you. It smells as if it's gone off—if that's possible with sherry.

Peggy Oh no, it isn't possible, is it? (*She cannot keep the alarm out of her face*)

Julian (*suspiciously*) Have you tried it?

Peggy Yes, look—my glass is nearly empty.

Julian Let me see you finish it up.

Peggy Certainly. (*With an effort, she drains her glass*)

Julian watches her with a cunning smile, but does not drink

You see, it's all right. Quite nice, in fact. Still, if you don't want it, it doesn't matter.

Julian (*rising casually and wandering up to the sideboard*) Oh, I'm just being fussy, really. (*With his back to her he tips his drink into a plant-pot on the sideboard, pretends to drink, and turns to face her*) No, it's quite nice as you say once it goes down. I think I'll have another one, if you don't mind.

Peggy (*relieved*) Not at all.

Julian (*pouring himself another drink, pretending to drink some of it, and coming back to the table*) I must say I regret having to leave here. I was beginning to enjoy myself. You're an interesting family—very interesting. Now is the cheque ready for me?

Peggy Yes, here it is. (*She hands it to him*)

Julian (*taking it and looking at it with interest, then putting it in his inside pocket*) Then I'll go.

Peggy Not yet ... (*She rises*)

Julian Why ever not?

Peggy I—I want to talk to you about something, ask your advice ...

Julian Well, I suppose I can spare a few minutes for a friend. (*He sits down on the settee*)

Peggy (*stalling for time*) It's about Howard ...

Julian Oh yes—Howard.

Peggy He's walked out on me. After all I've done for him.

Julian Don't worry, dear. I'm sure he'll come back when you start flashing your money about. He's no fool! (*He yawns exaggeratedly*)

Peggy Are you feeling tired?

Julian Yes, a bit. I can't think why. I almost feel like dropping off. (*He yawns again and half-closes his eyes*)

Peggy stands watching him hopefully. After a moment, his head slumps. He appears to be asleep. She creeps over to him and sitting down beside him on the settee touches him gently

Peggy Mr Fudge—Mr Fudge ...

He does not respond. She puts her hand inside his jacket pocket to find the cheque. She has it in her hands when suddenly his eyes open. He sits up and grabs her hand. She gasps with horror

Julian Just as I thought. Trying to see me off, were you? Wanted your money back, and then what—what were you going to do with me?

Peggy Nothing, nothing. You're mistaken.

Julian There was something in that drink, wasn't there? Something to make me pass out like a light. But I didn't drink it, you see. I tipped it in the flower-pot. So much for your little plans!

Peggy You're quite wrong . . .

Julian What had you in mind? Wait until I'd dozed off and put a pillow over my head like you did with the old man, was that it? Because that stuff wouldn't have killed me right away, you know. One of the old boy's sedatives, wasn't it? They take time to act, they're not like strychnine.

Peggy I wasn't trying to . . .

Julian A nice little sleeping-drug. I should have known you'd try something like that. But it wouldn't have killed me, you know, not that small quantity. Quite a nice, quiet death, actually, if you take enough. You sink slowly into an irreversible coma. Your body temperature gets lower and lower until you just fade away. Quite pleasant—as death goes. But I'm not ready to die yet, you see. I've got too many nice old gentlemen to look after. So what were you going to do with me, eh? Smother me to death while I slept? And then what? What were you going to do with the body? (*He grips her wrist hard*)

Peggy Let go of me—you're hurting me!

Julian Hurt you—so I should hurt you. (*He twists her arm*) Come on, tell me what you were going to do with me? I'd like to know.

Peggy (*gasping*) Dump you in the river—that's what . . .

Julian (*amused*) How were you going to manage that?

Peggy (*rubbing her wrist and arm*) I—I was going to put you in the wheel-chair and wait until dark and then take you down to the river . . .

Julian And tip me in? (*Scoffing*) What a desperate plan! You don't really think it would have worked?

Peggy I don't know. I don't care. I just had to get rid of you.

Julian I suppose you thought you'd committed one murder—why not another?

Peggy I—I resented giving you any of my money, that's all.

Julian You'll resent it even more when I tell you my price has now doubled.

Peggy Doubled?

Julian Of course. You've attempted to murder me. That's worth at least ten thousand pounds, wouldn't you say?

Peggy I won't pay you any more.

Julian Then I'll take that little brown bottle down to the police station and ask them to analyse it. You try to explain to *them* what you had in mind when you invited me to have a sherry.

Peggy (*moving to the table and sitting*) All right, then, but it isn't fair! (*She begins to write out another cheque*) I didn't really mean it, I didn't want to kill you. You forced me into it.

Julian (*sneering*) Forced you into it? I suppose I forced you into the other one, too.

Peggy (*wearily*) No, that was due to circumstances beyond my control.

Julian That's a very novel defence. "I'm sorry, me Lud, I didn't mean to kill the old bugger. It was due to circumstances beyond my control."

Peggy (*tearfully*) Stop making fun of me. I'm at the end of my tether. (*She tears the cheque out of the book*)

Julian (*taking it*) Thanks very much. You won't really notice it, will you? Not with the amount you've got.

Peggy (*picking up the Will from the table*) But I don't want it—I don't want any of it. I don't want my sisters to hate me! (*Suddenly she tears the Will up and scatters the pieces about*) There, now, I haven't got anything. Now try and claim it!

Julian Silly girl! Without that Will, the previous one would become valid. So, if the money is divided three ways, I think you've just got enough to pay me off. (*He puts the cheque away carefully*) Very kind of you I must say, but you've left yourself with nothing!

Peggy (*bitterly*) I don't care. I don't care. I'm sick of it all.

Julian (*with mock sympathy*) You have been rather foolish, my dear. Now you've got no money and no man! Never mind, your luck is bound to change! Look on the bright side, I always say. I needn't prolong my visit. I've got what I came for—and more besides. (*He goes towards the hall door*) I must say—it's been very nice knowing you!

Peggy You don't care what happens to me, do you? You might find it difficult to cash those cheques if I were dead.

Julian But you're not, are you? Nor likely to be. At least you look very healthy to me. I would give you a piece of advice, though, and that's to make yourself a strong cup of coffee, otherwise that little sip of sherry you took might make you sleepy all day. But it won't do more than that, not unless you decide to drink some more, that is.

Peggy I might just do that!

Julian I don't think so. You're much too resourceful to give up so easily. I must admit to a sneaking regard for you—despite everything. I like desperate, daring people. They're the winners in this world, you know. At least that's always been my experience. Well, I must be off. Cheeribye! You never know our paths may cross again some time!

Julian smiles smugly and goes off through the hall. The front door slams

Peggy (*in despair*) Oh God—oh God . . . (*She puts her head in her hands and begins to sob*)

The knocking starts, softly at first—the noise the old man used to make on the floor with his stick. Peggy looks up slowly in horror. She stares at the door

No—no . . . (*She gets up from her chair and backs away, then, as the noise increases in volume she runs across the room and puts the wheelchair hard against the door*)

The noise increases

It can't be—it can't be . . . (*She backs away from the door with her hands over her ears. After a moment she takes them away*)

The noise continues. With a sudden impetuous decision she goes to the sideboard, takes out the box of drugs, selects a bottle of tablets, and takes them and the sherry to the table. She pours herself a drink with shaking hands, takes a handful of tablets, and washes them down with the doctored sherry. She sits at the table and pours herself another glass, and then another. The knocking continues. Peggy is weeping and terrified. Gradually she loses consciousness. She slumps forward on to the table. The knocking dies away

After a pause, the hall door is slowly pushed open. Mrs Moore looks in

Mrs Moore I wondered why I couldn't open that door. What a funny place to leave the old man's wheel-chair! (*She moves the chair and comes into the room*) I just popped in to tidy up. I didn't know you'd be 'ere. (*She goes to Peggy*) Peggy—are you all right, duck? (*She pushes Peggy back in the chair*)

Peggy's head lolls forward, she groans

'Ere, what's this? Fast asleep at this time in the morning? (*She looks at the sherry decanter*) I do believe you've been drinking. Who'd a' thought it? Dead drunk! (*She shakes her head*) Tut, tut—well I never! It's all been too much for you, these last few days. I don't blame you, I really don't. Never you mind, duck. Your secret will be safe with me. (*She looks round and, seeing the rug in the wheel-chair, goes and brings it to wrap round Peggy*) There you are, you sleep it off, dear. I won't disturb you, I promise. You can sleep to Kingdom Come if you like. In fact, I'll pretend I wasn't here at all. I'll just go back home and come in again tomorrow. Sleep tight, my dear. God knows, you need it!

Mrs Moore goes off through the hall. The front door slams

Gradually the knocking comes again, rising to a crescendo, as—

the CURTAIN falls

Note: the last bout of knocking can be amplified and put through loud-speakers to give it an eerie, echoing sound

FURNITURE AND PROPERTY LIST

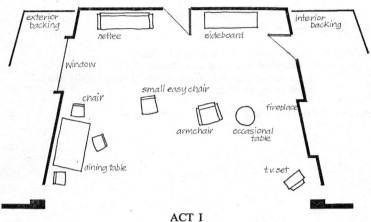

ACT I

SCENE 1

On stage: Armchair
Small easy chair
3 upright chairs
Settee. *On it:* cushions
Sideboard. *On it:* framed photographs, plant-pot, dressing. *In drawers:* crockery, cutlery, tablecloth
Occasional table
Dining-table
Over fireplace: mirror. *Beside it:* metal wastepaper-basket
On mantelpiece: clock, ornaments, matches, ashtray
Fireguard
Carpet
Window curtains

Off stage: Doorslam and knocker (practical, for actors)
Basket of shopping **(Peggy)**
Hot-water bottle **(Julie)**
Sponge-bag with curlers **(Babs)**
Tray with 4 cups of tea, saucers, spoons **(Peggy)**
Tray with covered dish, salt, pepper, bread, butter **(Peggy)**
Brief envelope with Will **(Peggy)**

Personal: **Babs:** handbag with cigarettes and matches
Julie: handbag with four £5 notes
Peggy: engagement ring

SCENE 2

Strike: Tea things
              Cutlery, etc., back to sideboard
              Pills
              Peggy's handbag
              Burnt Will

Set: Wheel-chair with rug and pillow
              Main armchair against wall

Off stage: Pills and glass of water on tray **(Julian)**
              Mr Dalrymple's hat and coat **(Julian)**
              Tray with jug of coffee, cream, 3 cups, 3 saucers **(Mrs Moore)**
              Bag of shopping **(Peggy)**

Personal: **Peggy:** handbag with cigarettes and matches

ACT II

SCENE 1

Strike: Glass of water and pills
              Coffee things
              Crockery, etc., back to sideboard

Set: Armchair in original position
              Magazine on occasional table

Personal: **Peggy:** wristwatch

SCENE 2

Strike: Wheel-chair

Set: Armchair beside sideboard
              Settee down into room
              Tray with sherry decanter and 6 glasses on sideboard

Off stage: Plate of sandwiches, plate of cakes **(Mrs Moore)**
              Envelope containing Will **(Peggy)**
              2 suitcases **(Julie)**
              Envelope containing Will **(Julian)**

Personal: **Babs:** handkerchief

ACT II

Strike: **Peggy**'s hat
Cakes and sandwiches
Dirty sherry glasses

Set: **Babs**'s handbag with cigarettes and matches on table
Clean sherry glasses

Off stage: Cup of tea **(Babs)**
Morning paper **(Howard)**
Cup of tea **(Howard)**
2 cups of tea **(Babs)**
Wheel-chair. *On it:* old clothes, rug, cardboard box containing pills
   and liquid medicines **(Babs)**
Slice of toast and glass of milk **(Babs)**
Envelope with Will **(Julian)**

Personal: **Peggy:** handbag with cheque-book and pen

LIGHTING PLOT

Property fittings required: pendant or wall brackets
Interior. A living-room. The same scene throughout

ACT I. SCENE 1   Day
To open: Effect of September afternoon light
No cues

ACT I. SCENE 2   Day
To open: Effect of late September morning light
No cues

ACT II. SCENE 1   Evening
To open: Curtains closed, interior lighting on
Cue 1   **Peggy:** "... it isn't fair!"   (Page 34)
                  Pause, then bring up TV flicker effect

ACT II. SCENE 2   Day
To open: Effect of late September afternoon
No cues

ACT III   Day
To open: As Act I, Scene 2
No cues

EFFECTS PLOT

ACT I

SCENE 1

SCENE 2

No cues

ACT II

SCENE 1

SCENE 2

ACT III